# A Busy Parent's Guide to a Meaningful Lent

# A Busy Parent's Guide to a Meaningful Lent

MARIA C. MORROW

Our Sunday Visitor
Huntington, Indiana

*Nihil Obstat*
Msgr. Michael Heintz, Ph.D.
*Censor Librorum*

*Imprimatur*
✠ Kevin C. Rhoades
Bishop of Fort Wayne-South Bend
August 14, 2020

The *Nihil Obstat* and *Imprimatur* are official declarations that a book is free from doctrinal or moral error. It is not implied that those who have granted the *Nihil Obstat* and *Imprimatur* agree with the contents, opinions, or statements expressed.



25 24 23 22 21 20     1 2 3 4 5 6 7 8 9



Our Sunday Visitor Publishing Division
Our Sunday Visitor, Inc.
200 Noll Plaza
Huntington, IN 46750
1-800-348-2440

ISBN: 978-1-68192-609-4 (Inventory No. T2474)
1. RELIGION—Holidays—Easter & Lent.
2. RELIGION—Christian Life—Family.
3. RELIGION—Christianity—Catholic.

eISBN: 978-1-68192-610-0
LCCN: 2020943333

Cover and interior: Lindsey Riesen
Cover art: Restored Traditions

Printed in the United States of America

Dedicated with love to my parents,
Robert and Kathryn Feilmeyer,
whose faithfulness and love were always inspiring
and whose sacrifices I never appreciated
until I had children.

# TABLE OF CONTENTS

BEFORE LENT BEGINS
*How to Use This Book*
9

ASH WEDNESDAY AND BEYOND
*The Guarantee of Success (and Failure)*
19

FIRST WEEK OF LENT
*Cultivating a God's-Eye View*
35

SECOND WEEK OF LENT
*Letting Go of Control*
67

THIRD WEEK OF LENT
*Seeking and Receiving*
97

FOURTH WEEK OF LENT
*The Generosity and Abundance of God's Love*
129

FIFTH WEEK OF LENT
*Embracing Difficulty and Suffering*
159

HOLY WEEK AND EASTER
*Sharing in the Life and Death of Jesus*
189

APPENDIX
*Feasts and Solemnities of Lent*
219

ACKNOWLEDGMENTS
239

# BEFORE LENT BEGINS

## *How to Use This Book*

My first child was due on Easter Monday. I will never forget my reaction when my husband asked me what I was thinking about doing for Lent that year. I responded sarcastically, "Gosh, I was thinking about weighing an extra thirty pounds, not being able to sleep at night, tripling my trips to the bathroom, living with constant heartburn, limiting my wardrobe to just a few outfits, getting out of breath walking up the steps, having swollen feet, and possibly … maybe … fitting in labor and a delivery." My newbie husband (God bless him) said, "Ha! No, really, what are you giving up?"

That probably was not the best response to an uncomfortable woman in the final weeks of her first pregnancy! But my response to his initial question wasn't the best, either. The thought of taking on any further sacrifices was … unpleasant, to say the least. But I did not realize that this combination of inconveniences caused by children and the call to Lenten penance was only the beginning. Since the birth of my Easter Friday baby, I have had more than a decade's worth of Lents as a parent, and they have each been difficult in their own unexpected ways.

However, while pregnancy and parenting both present their own very challenging circumstances, we parents cannot just give up on Lent, much like we should not give up on having a prayer life when it becomes harder to integrate thanks to raising a family. Rather than seeing an "either-or" conflict, we should see this as a "both-and" where we stand to benefit. Living Lent well can help us be better and holier parents. Striving to be better and holier parents can help us to live Lent well. So, let's recognize that whatever the challenges of our state of life, we are still being called to participate in this season of Lent!

**Lenten Penance in the Past and Present**

In years past, the whole Church fasted for all of the forty days of Lent. Yes, you read that right: all the forty days of Lent, not just Ash Wednesday and Good Friday. Additional Lenten resolutions were often added to this, and each person chose some sacrifice that was particularly meaningful for them. Beginning with the Lent of 1967, however, obligatory daily fasting was limited to Ash Wednesday and Good Friday, and the emphasis instead fell on the individually chosen Lenten resolutions. The main motivation for the bishops' change was to provide a better opportunity for personal Lenten sacrifices, since the spiritual life is not one-size-fits-all. The downside to this change was a lack of social support, the loss of the sense that we're all in this together, joining in the exact same fast. But the potential benefit is that we are able to discern what Lenten practices might be best in bringing us closer to God as we prepare for Easter.

**Do Something!**

The constant sacrifices of parenting can make it seem like Lent is somehow adding insult to injury! On top of all the predictable (laundry, meals, fighting kids) and unpredictable (sudden injury or illness) daily difficulties of life, we are asked to take on some voluntary penance during this season of Lent. This is not the time to play the spiritual hero or the somber martyr. The Lenten resolutions of parents should not make life miserable for the kids. After all, as parenting experts are constantly reminding us (as if there wasn't enough pressure!), we are always modeling for our children. It's ok for penance to be hard, even if our kids notice that. But it shouldn't make us into hangry monsters. That won't be a good model of how to do a Lenten resolution. Nonetheless, we should try to do something voluntarily that reminds us (and hopefully shows our children) that we are living a bit differently in Lent than we do otherwise.

## Choosing a Lenten Resolution: The Traditional Triad

In choosing a Lenten resolution, it is helpful to recall the traditional triad of Lenten penances: prayer, fasting, and almsgiving. These can take many different forms, and incorporating all three into Lenten observance is ideal.

### *Almsgiving*

Biblical scholar Gary Anderson has written beautifully and convincingly on the importance of almsgiving in the history of the Church.* The willingness to share our resources with those in need is an indication of our trust in God to provide for us. It also calls to mind the generosity of God in giving us everything, most especially his son, Jesus. We are called to imitate that generosity. Almsgiving reminds us that all we have comes from God, and we should share that selflessly with those around us, remembering the poor who suffer from lack of resources. And yet, almsgiving is perhaps the most neglected of the Lenten practices, and often seems daunting or impossible. After all, with a house full of kids,

* Gary Anderson, *Sin: A History*.

how do we have time to minister to those in need?

One idea is to look for easily available opportunities, such as those provided by parishes. Our churches often provide occasions for almsgiving through food pantries, sandwich ministries, etc. These are wonderful weekly opportunities for feeding the hungry in a tangible way; grab a couple of cans of tuna on the way to Sunday Mass to add to the food pantry. It may not be much, but it is something. Another similar idea is to pick up a bag of groceries during your usual shopping trip, and drop it off at a shelter; this doesn't take too much time out of a busy week and is a great way of providing direct assistance to those in need.

Beggars are not commonplace everywhere, but if you do live in a place where you might be able to give food or a few dollars directly to people in need, this can be a good almsgiving practice as well. When my family visits New York City, we try to make up one giveaway bag for each of our kids, containing a few food items and a few dollars for them to hand to the poor that we encounter on the streets. Being aware of the needs of more immediate friends and acquaintances is also important. Recently I learned that someone I saw regularly at the swimming pool was going through a hard financial time with unemployment and a foreclosure on her house. After that, I tried to keep a little cash in my wallet that I could just hand to her when I saw her (or leave anonymously in her swim bag or locker).

Finally, there are many organizations who benefit greatly from donations as they do their work for the poor. The Lenten rice boxes provided at churches aid Catholic Relief Services worldwide, while also educating us about the people who benefit from CRS. There are many other local organizations, such as pregnant women's shelters, that also do great work and are always in need of resources. This almsgiving often feels more indirect, but it also can encourage us to learn more about various ministries and those in need both locally and globally.

Again, it can feel overwhelming to fit almsgiving into a busy family household. Realistically, we probably can't manage to do the heroic almsgiving and corporal works of mercy for the poor that we might do if we were single and childless. However, there usually is something we can do — and, even better, do in a way that involves our children. Starting off the season of Lent with a desire to practice almsgiving will help us to be aware of the opportunities we are presented throughout our preparation for Easter. Such almsgiving may not be a daily sort of resolution, but it can be weekly or even just a few times during Lent.

*Fasting*

Fasting is probably the Lenten practice with which we are most familiar, even if the "fasting" we do now during Lent is not the daily fasting of Catholics prior to 1967. Fasting today is more likely to take the form of "giving up" something that we like. At its most basic, fasting is about food, and there is great diversity in the foods that people fast from during Lent. This makes sense, as certain people have a weakness for certain kinds of foods. Giving up soda, sweets, or eating between meals can all have the effect of making us aware of our creature comforts and reminding us that only God can satisfy.

If you find it burdensome to determine what best to give up, you might consider looking to past traditions of the Church. Abstinence from meat, dairy, and eggs throughout the season of Lent was required for many centuries in Church practice. Giving up all three of those may seem daunting, but variations on this can be incorporated easily. For example, you might want to give up just red meat or limit your meat intake to one meal a day. You might give up butter on your toast or cream in your coffee. This kind of abstinence can also be incorporated into family life; the parent in charge of mealtimes can limit meat or dairy throughout Lent.

Likewise, although fasting can seem daunting, you might

consider a commitment to not eating between meals during the season of Lent. The sensation of hunger is a powerful reminder that only God can satisfy us; earthly food is passing. Of course, we need to be careful when selecting Lenten resolutions such as these. My mom friends and I always talk about how fasting days often become "yelling at kids" days. So it's important to start a fasting day by recognizing that it may affect your patience with your kids. If times of low blood sugar bring out a short temper, especially if you have young children, it's better not to do this kind of sacrifice. You may want to try it for a few days, but be willing to change if you see it is more naturally harmful than supernaturally beneficial! Having a song or prayer to return to when feeling short-tempered can help, as well as not trying to play the hero by getting lots of stuff done or doing a fun/overwhelming trip to the zoo.

While fasting is primarily tied to food, in our world today, fasting from technology can also be helpful for our spiritual life during Lent. This, again, can take many forms. Perhaps it means a break from social media, or restrictions on online shopping or checking email. Putting our phones on grayscale can help curb and increase thoughtfulness in our phone use. We may want to incorporate time limits for entertainment and renew efforts toward downtime from our screens. All of these practices can reduce distraction and noise in our lives, helping us to be more focused and attentive during the season of Lent. This can allow us to become more responsive to God, as well as more observant and patient with our children.

Also, it's good to remember that we encounter days within the season of Lent that are not days of penance. The Solemnity of Saint Joseph (March 19) and the Annunciation (March 25), when they fall on ordinary weekdays of Lent, are numbered among the highest ranking feast days in the Church and thus are not obligatory days of penance. So also, every Sunday of Lent is a solemnity. You may choose to lighten your penance on these feasts, to mark their significance and make these days feel different.

*Prayer*

One of the many challenges faced by us as busy parents is how to have a solid prayer life, especially when time is short and children are present. For a parent, it takes creativity, sacrifice, and flexibility, as well as trial and error, to find space and time for prayer. My husband and I have made it a priority to each attend daily Mass; it requires an early morning schedule, but has been unbelievably valuable. I treasure that half hour to myself and find it strengthens me for the day. And although it's not an ideal scenario perhaps, I've come to depend on saying my Rosary during a morning walk or run, just as my husband counts on his morning commute to fit in prayer time. You might find it difficult or impossible to find time away from children for prayer such as Eucharistic adoration or daily Mass, and that's okay. It can be great to involve children in these types of prayer, but that can also be stressful in a way that does not feel prayerful. Fortunately, there are many other ways to pray, for those who are unable to find time alone or unenthusiastic about bringing children to communal (mostly silent) times of prayer.

And that is where this book comes into play. My aim is to provide an opportunity for us as parents to incorporate daily prayer throughout Lent, with added suggestions for observing Lent in ways — including almsgiving and fasting — that are appropriate and realistic for parents. Consider it a retreat of sorts, providing Scripture readings from the daily Mass texts, along with questions for further reflection throughout each day and week of Lent. This focused prayer will help us busy parents to make the most of Lent in the midst of family life.

**Using This Book**

Ideally, these daily reflections should be read at the beginning of the day — if not upon awakening, then at the first opportunity. Reading the reflections should only take a few minutes, and then you'll need just a few more minutes for prayerfully considering the questions and thinking about how to reflect on them further throughout the day. It may seem an unconventional way to do a Lenten "retreat," but it is an achievable way to make the season of Lent more prayerful. If you have more time, whether first thing or later in the day, I'd invite you also to read the Mass readings for each day, which are listed prior to the reflection. The Lenten Sunday readings change on a three-year cycle, so you will find different reflections for years A, B, and C.

Each day begins with a title that indicates the theme of the reflection. Following this you will find five sections: Read, Reflect, Pray, Ponder, Do. "Read" provides a listing of the Scripture readings from the Mass for that day, if you have time to read the full readings prior to the reflection.

Under "Reflect" you will find a brief reflection that relates these readings to the life of parents, proposing ways that we might integrate family life with the season of Lent.

In the "Pray" section you'll have the opportunity to adopt a brief prayer, often biblically based from the day's readings, to return to throughout the day. During those times when we feel busiest and have no time for ourselves, having a one-line prayer to remember helps us live the season of Lent throughout the whole day.

In the "Ponder" section you will find questions related to the readings and the reflection. You might use these questions to guide further reflections throughout the day, to pray about in a moment of silence, to inspire journaling, or to share in discussion with friends.

Finally, in the "Do" section, I have included a suggested Catholic practice, such as a morning offering, for each week. These practices are brief and "easy," in the sense that we can incorporate them without big changes; nonetheless, they can genuinely help renew our spiritual life, especially when we are struggling with finding time for prayer.

## Difficult but Not Impossible

Father Walter Ciszek was a Polish-American Jesuit priest imprisoned in a Siberian labor camp during World War II and the Cold War. He worked long hours every day, shoveling coal or digging ditches in below-freezing temperatures. Father Ciszek realized that he would not be able to have a silent retreat, as he had in years past, where he focused on the Ignatian spiritual exercises. But while he could not accomplish the peaceful ideal, he recognized that he was still able to do the Ignatian spiritual exercises, and direct others in them, even in the midst of the labor camp. Digging ditches and shoveling coal isn't what normally jumps to mind for most people when they hear the word "retreat," yet Ciszek ministered in these conditions, helping people live prayerfully in the midst of stressful and difficult working conditions by keeping their minds attentive to spiritual matters.

Hopefully our experience of parenting is not quite as dire as a Siberian labor camp! But like Father Ciszek, we parents can't easily get away from it all in order to connect with God in silence. We live our Lent in the midst of our responsibilities to our families. We can still be prayerfully attentive to God's work and God's will if we find a way to make an effort. May this book be a helpful aid to you in the journey of this Lent!

# ASH WEDNESDAY AND BEYOND

*The Guarantee of Success (and Failure)*

# ASH WEDNESDAY AND BEYOND

This is a day of fasting and abstinence from meat. A fast day allows for two small snacks, not totaling a full meal, and one full meal. Fish and dairy are allowed on days of abstinence, as are liquids throughout the day. This is also the first day for observing one's voluntary Lenten resolution. Note that the Church exempts women who are pregnant or breastfeeding, as well as those with certain medical conditions, from these regulations.

## Read

- Joel 2:12–18
- Psalm: 51:3–4, 5–6AB, 12–13, 14, and 17

  R. Be merciful, O Lord, for we have sinned.
- 2 Corinthians 5:20–6:2
- Matthew 6:1–6, 16–18

## Reflect

As parents, it is easy to procrastinate on our spiritual lives. We seem always to have more pressing matters, from laundry to soccer games to bedtime routines. For this reason, the liturgical seasons of the Church are a great gift to us. Whether we feel ready or not, Lent has begun. Today is Ash Wednesday, and as the second reading from 2 Corinthians tells us, "Behold, now is a very acceptable time; behold, now is the day of salvation" (2 Cor 6:2).

Embracing this season of Lent does not mean letting go or ignoring all of our family responsibilities. In fact, quite the opposite! Now is the time to see our work as parents in a spiritual light.

The life of parenting is intrinsically a life of service; we serve our children and society in the work we do in the home. More importantly, however, we serve God in our actions as parents.

This is an important point to reflect on during Lent. Maybe you regret that you don't have time to observe Lent as you did in earlier (childless) days, or perhaps you've never been that into Lent. Today, on Ash Wednesday, we make every effort to get to church and receive ashes, but even this annual routine can feel challenging with young children in tow. The fasting of Ash Wednesday can be a struggle as well; maintaining patience in the home while fasting is not an easy thing to do.

However, this is a new beginning. Today we have a great opportunity to recognize that God wants us to live Lent just as we are, as parents. It is here that our freedom lies: doing God's will in the moment, in the life he has given us. When we fail to see our lives this way, we easily become resentful. We may go through the motions of parenting, even in all the right ways, but without the right intentions. And we may adhere to Church teachings without the passion that indicates a real love of God.

This attitude is not unlike that found in today's Gospel reading, where we hear the instructions: "Take care not to perform righteous deeds in order that people may see them" (Mt 6:1). Our Lord does not want us to forgo righteous deeds. Rather, he wants us to attend to our intentions, and amend them when necessary. Likewise, the main point of parenting is not putting on an impressive show for others; it is offering our very lives to God.

How often do we fail in this? All the time. We are almost guaranteed failure, to some degree, as we raise our children. Whether because we are sleep deprived, or overwhelmed, or uncertain in a particular situation, we may not always know or make the right decisions as parents. We may sometimes get distracted from doing God's will by the pressures put on us by society. What a gift Lent is to us! It is a time to recognize all the ways we fail and to reach out to God in humility, asking to be reconciled to God. We cannot do it on our own. We can never earn our own salvation. But the Lord wants to give us the grace to do his will in every moment, from making a meal for the family to picking up dirty socks off the floor. When we take up our crosses, uniting them to Christ during this season of Lent, we find that even our many failures guarantee our eventual success, our eternal life and sharing in Jesus' resurrection.

**Pray**

Have mercy on me, God, in accord with your merciful love; in your abundant compassion blot out my transgressions. (Psalm 51:3)

**Ponder**

- Where have I been procrastinating or using my parenting responsibilities as excuses in my spiritual life? How can I be proactive during this season of Lent, recognizing it as "the acceptable time"?
- How will my Lenten resolution remind me of God's call to repentance?
- How will I fast today in a way that does not negatively affect my children but does help me grow spiritually? Hint: Be proactive in recognizing the potential for being short of patience while fasting, and plan for low-key activities and prayer to help stay calm.

**Do**

*This Week: Pray a Morning Offering*

A morning offering prayer is a traditional Catholic practice to offer the day's work to God. As parents who face struggles every day and often forget that we do this work to serve God, a morning offering provides a way of beginning the day in God's service. There are many beautiful traditional morning offering prayers, and using our own words also works well. If you have not already been praying a morning offering, use this week to learn one and aim to pray it every morning upon awakening.

Here is one example of a morning offering:

> God, I offer to you all that I am and all that I do this day, in reparation for my sins, for the good of my family and friends, with the help of the angels and saints, and most especially your Blessed Mother. Amen.

# THURSDAY AFTER ASH WEDNESDAY

## Read

- Deuteronomy 30:15–20
- Psalm 1:1–2, 3, 4, and 6
  R. Blessed are they who hope in the Lord.
- Luke 9:22–25

## Reflect

Today's first reading and Gospel both appear to present choices. In the reading from Deuteronomy, Moses speaks to the Israelites in the desert, asking them to "choose life" over death by deciding to love God and follow God's commandments, rather than adoring and serving other gods.

Jesus takes this one step further, telling his disciples that the way to choose life is to lose it for his sake. The revelation of the person of Jesus presents us with a new way of loving God: following Jesus, even when that means suffering, rejection, and death.

It may seem a grim revision of Moses' call to choose life; but in fact, it is the opposite. Choosing death by following Jesus is ultimately a choice for life, a choice to share in the eternal life of Jesus' resurrection. This paradox of choosing death in order to choose life confronts us all in daily life, as we are presented with many crosses that we would rather leave behind than take up.

Our first challenge, then, is to amend our will so that we want to choose death in order to choose life, to desire the crosses and want to follow Jesus. And this is where we can recognize a great blessing in our lives as parents. Each day we are given various crosses that are truly unavoidable: mopping the spilled milk from the ground, rearranging a schedule to take a sick kid to the doctor, losing sleep as a teething baby pulls an all-nighter, hearing criticisms of others in regard to our children, disciplining fighting siblings, dealing with whining, etc.

Our second challenge is to identify these particular difficulties and offer them specifically as crosses. After all, parents everywhere make these same sorts of necessary sacrifices, more or less willingly. What makes the Christian approach different is the end we envision. Parenting is not simply about raising children, or even raising children well. It is about following Jesus, taking up the cross, choosing death so that we can share in eternal life, and, hopefully, share that eternal life with our children.

It's easy to fall into a grumbling perspective about our lack of choice as parents. So much of every single day with children seems to reflect our complete lack of choice, the inability to follow our own will and pursue our own desires. And yet, that's exactly where the choice comes in; we can embrace this as God's will. We have to remind ourselves that we want to take up Jesus' cross, and that the difficulties of parenting represent important opportunities to do that.

Lent is an ideal time to identify the little dissatisfactions that come with not having everything our own way in our lives as parents. We really are not in control, as our little people constantly seem to demonstrate. And as much as we strive to do God's will, taking up the cross and following Jesus, we can also recognize that we frequently fail at this.

Nor should we be surprised. The season of Lent teaches us that we aren't perfect. Even our best intentions often fall through. We finally lose our patience with the kids at the end of a hard day. We can't spare a smile for a spouse after awakening too early from a sleep-deprived night. Having misbehaving children at Sunday Mass puts us in a far too angry state of mind. We may tell ourselves that we want to take up the cross of Christ, but when it falls in our path, we spontaneously react, "No! Not now! Not this cross!"

Thank God, praise God, that we are not responsible for our own salvation! We must rely on Jesus more and more during this season of Lent. We cannot take up our cross and save the world through our own death. We can only depend on his cross, and unite our difficulties to that cross of Christ. When we recognize and even accept our continual challenges and failures, we are granted the freedom to succeed by sharing in Christ's victory.

## Pray

Take up your cross and follow me. (see Luke 9:23)

## Ponder

- How is God calling me to "choose death" in my responsibilities to my family? What is one concrete way that I can put my personal preferences aside in order to prioritize others?
- What crosses is God asking me to embrace in this season of Lent?
- What prayers or acts would help me to unite my struggles to the cross of Christ?

## Do

*This Week: Pray a Morning Offering*

Identifying our parenting challenges as crosses to embrace is hard. We often forget that we want to do everything for God. Praying the morning offering is an excellent way to establish, right when we wake up, that this day is for God. And often, if we recall this intention before we begin our daily duties, we will also remember it throughout the day. Even if we don't recall it frequently, making the intention at the beginning of the day consecrates the whole day, no matter what.

# FRIDAY AFTER ASH WEDNESDAY

All Catholics are required to abstain from meat on ordinary Fridays of Lent; pregnant or nursing women and those who suffer from chronic physical or mental illness are exempt from this obligation, but encouraged to participate in abstinence from meat.

### Read

- Isaiah 58:1–9A
- Psalm 51:3–4, 5–6AB, 18–19
  R. A heart contrite and humbled, O God, you will not spurn.
- Matthew 9:14–15

### Reflect

Today, on this first Friday of our Lenten season, we are confronted with the important place held by fasting in our tradition. In our contemporary age, this may seem quite foreign. After all, Catholics are now bound to fast only on two days of the entire year: Ash Wednesday and Good Friday. And these fast days do allow for one full meal, as well as two smaller snacks during the day. As recently as 1965, however, Catholics were expected to keep this fast on every single day of Lent (excepting solemnities such as Sundays).

Although we are not required to fast today, the Fridays of Lent are days of abstinence from meat. This small sacrifice reminds us of Christ's death on Good Friday and provides a way of marking this day as different from others, even different from those other days of Lent.

Fasting is a remarkable practice that can be a powerful reminder of our dependence on God and the spiritual meaning of our lives beyond our physical bodies. However, what we see in the first reading from the prophet Isaiah is that fasting can also become a source of problematic pride, a way of justifying ourselves and our behavior, at the expense of those around us in need.

The strict fasting practice that Isaiah has in mind is largely not observed by us today, as our actual fasting is quite minimal. Nonetheless, we may have experienced a certain ambivalence when it comes to sharing our Lenten resolution with others. Some prefer to hide it from others, keeping it "secret." And it's true that when we give voice to our chosen Lenten penance, we can appear to be (or feel to be) bragging about what a big sacrifice we are making. But on the other hand, when we keep it private, that also may become a source of pride to us: Not only are we making a big sacrifice, but we also are so much holier because we aren't mentioning it to anyone!

How hard it is to approach a season of penance in a true spirit of repentance! We may fail in our Lenten resolution and feel we haven't done our duty. Or we may succeed in keeping our resolution and feel a large amount of pride at our success, then realizing that this is its own sort of failure. We are caught, not unlike those Isaiah describes in the first reading. Those who focus on correct observance may fail to see the bigger picture; they may demand to receive that which they see as their due.

Add in the ordinary stress of day-to-day parenting and those necessary sacrifices that accompany it, and we may ask ourselves why we should even bother with Lenten resolutions. Isn't life tough enough? Don't I already live a daily life of sacrifice and penance? Doesn't trying to fast cause more problems than it solves?

Yes, there are risks whenever we undertake penance. Once more, failure seems imminent. And yet again, it is in this failure that we can find success. After all, our Lenten resolutions aren't really about us. They are about God, letting God work in us, and loving God by making an intentional effort. Whether we fail or succeed, whether we tell the world or keep it private, whether we proceed out of habit or sometimes feel contrition for our sins, we are likely to practice penance imperfectly. But that is no reason to give it up. Like a loving parent who understands the weaknesses of his children, God is pleased with the effort of those who persist in trying to do his will.

## Pray

Have mercy on me, God, in accord with your merciful love; in your abundant compassion blot out my transgressions. (Psalm 51:3)

## Ponder

- When I feel hypocritical, what is a practical way that I can share that with God and make a concrete effort to correct my actions?
- What can I do to remind myself that my Lenten resolution is not about me and my abilities and willpower, but about offering a sacrifice to God?
- How can I incorporate my Lenten resolution into my life without it becoming a burden for my family?

## Do

*This Week: Pray a Morning Offering*

All that we do each day should be done for God, and that includes the penance of this Friday! Especially because of the way that Friday meat abstinence and our Lenten resolutions can become perfunctory and meaningless through repetition, a morning offering today can help us correctly to direct our actions toward the end of serving God on this particular day of penance. Today, let us focus on offering all of our work and sacrifices to God.

# SATURDAY AFTER ASH WEDNESDAY

## Read

- Isaiah 58:9B–14
- Psalm 86:1–2, 3–4, 5–6

  R. Teach me your way, O Lord, that I may walk in your truth.
- Luke 5:27–32

## Reflect

One powerful theme found throughout our Gospels is the eager willingness of some — although not all — to follow Jesus immediately. When we look at, for example, the tax collector Levi (Matthew) described in today's Gospel, we see that these quick responders to Jesus' invitation have a humility. They recognize that something important is missing from their lives. They acknowledge their sinfulness. They aren't afraid to turn to Jesus for answers because they recognize they just aren't making it on their own — even if the world regards them as successful.

This attitude of humility makes all the difference. In contrast to the Pharisees and scribes in today's Gospel, Levi is someone who recognizes that he is sick. "Those who are healthy do not need a physician, but the sick do. I have not come to call the righteous to repentance but sinners." These words of Jesus acknowledge that he is calling sinners such as Levi the tax collector. But they also imply that Jesus could be a physician for these scribes and Pharisees … if only they could recognize the ways they, too, are sick.

In order to gain healing, the sick have to recognize their illness. They have to seek a cure and be willing to bear with the necessary treatment in order to achieve health, even if this causes discomfort in the short-term. Particularly during this season of Lent, we too must acknowledge that we are sick in some ways and require the healing of that divine physician, Jesus. We must be willing to open our wounds to him, to recognize and confess our many sins and faults. If we continue to act as if everything is just fine, we are unlikely to receive that forgiveness and grace that we need for this journey of life.

One burden (and hence, gift) of parenting, is the constant knowledge of our stumbles. We easily become impatient. We get frustrated when our plans don't go our way because our children derail them — sometimes even purposefully! We can't seem to make time for prayer. We fail at consistent discipline. We get distracted by technology and aren't attentive enough to the family.

Yes, we fail. And if we can share these failures with God, and unite them to the cross of Christ, we can still be hopeful. It is only when we deny our sickness, as did the scribes and Pharisees, that we will not be open to a cure. If we embrace humility and acknowledge our dependence on the good Lord, we can truly repent of our sin, and illness will lead to healing.

## Pray

To you, Lord, I lift up my soul. (Psalm 86:4)

## Reflect

- How can I strive to practice generosity both with my children and with others around me in need of my resources?
- What am I grateful for today? How do I recognize God's generosity to me at this time?

- How am I sick and in need of healing?

**Do**

*This Week: Pray a Morning Offering*

It's easy for us parents to fall into the habit of "playing the martyr," constantly listing the sacrifices we make for our children and becoming resentful of the many tedious housekeeping and child-rearing tasks. Saying a morning offering helps correct this attitude. Each day we will have to do many tasks that we wouldn't necessarily choose, but when we offer all of our life and actions to God each day, we can see these sacrifices as a way both to appreciate and demonstrate the generosity of God.

# FIRST WEEK OF LENT

*Cultivating a God's-Eye View*

# FIRST SUNDAY OF LENT, YEAR A

## *Year A: 2023, 2026, 2029, 2032*

### Read

- Genesis 2:7–9, 3:1–7
- Psalm 51:3–4, 5–6, 12–13, 17
  R. Be merciful, O Lord, for we have sinned.
- Romans 5:12–19
- Matthew 4:1–11

### Reflect

This first Sunday of Lent provides us with two very well-known passages from Scripture: the fall of Adam and Eve from the book of Genesis, coupled with Matthew's Gospel passage describing Jesus' temptation by the Devil in the desert. They are meant to correspond, showing us the original sin of Adam and Eve, contrasting with Jesus' faithfulness when similarly confronted by Satan. Rather than trusting the directions of God for what was best, Adam and Eve chose to follow their own will at the suggestion of the Devil. Jesus, however, sees through the Devil's words, recognizing the falseness of his claims and holding fast to the will of the Father.

Although we are neither Adam or Eve, nor Jesus, these readings are intrinsically about us — about all humankind. We are the descendants of Adam and Eve, and we see around us the daily illustration of the pull of sin. We probably even recognize that inclination in our own lives; we prefer to follow our own will, to have life our way, pursuing the ends that we want. And we want to do this without consequences, failing to recognize that our will may not be that which is best for others, or even ourselves. This story of the fall of Adam and Eve shows that there simply are consequences when we decide to follow our own desires rather than God's instructions.

And yet again, failure is not the end of the story. The second reading from Paul's letter to the Romans bridges the two other readings, reminding us that we share in the reward for Jesus' obedience — not just as he faces down the temptations of the Devil, but also as he suffers and dies on the cross. Moreover, the consequences of Jesus' choices more than compensate for the losses we suffer through Adam and Eve. Paul uses the words "abundance" and "overflowing." This grace is our new inheritance; we are made righteous when we share in Christ's life.

Before our life as parents, we probably found it easier to follow our own will. If we felt like going out to dinner, we could just walk out the door and go. We could take up long-distance running without inconveniencing anyone. We could schedule volunteering or service times and keep those hours limited to what suited us best. Perhaps we approached these decisions with some degree of discernment and prayer, or perhaps decided the small stuff didn't take much reflection.

With the responsibility of family often comes the recognition that we have been somewhat selfish or self-centered in our choices. Suddenly, the consequences of our choices can be quite negative for those who depend on us. Rather than serving others for a few hours a week, we find ourselves constantly on duty, serving others 24-7. The newfound lack of choice can be startling and can even cause dismay for parents. Parents often seem less happy with their lives than others who don't have children.

Rather than seeing a constriction on our freedom, however, we are called to see a growth in our freedom. After all, freedom isn't about doing whatever we want, whenever we want. Freedom comes when we do God's will. We see that in Jesus fighting the temptations of the Devil and quoting the word of God as support. This is true freedom, whereas the free-will choice of Adam and Eve represented a slavery to sin.

Our goal, then, is to cultivate a God's-eye view of our life, rather than seeing life through our own perception. We may see the burdensome menial household tasks as something inhibiting our freedom; but from God's perspective, doing this work cheerfully for God helps us to grow in freedom. Getting up in the middle of the night to clean up a child's vomit is not something we want or would choose to do, but embracing this duty as God's will can help us become more free. Giving up some luxuries in order to pay the expenses of children can appear to others to be a sacrifice of happiness; but when we unite this sacrifice to Jesus' own sacrifices, we find ourselves happier than might make sense to an outside observer.

## Pray

Lord, you will open my lips; and my mouth will proclaim your praise. (Psalm 51:17)

## Reflect

- How well is my Lenten resolution working to bring me closer to God? Is there anything I should change about my resolution this week?
- What are some ways in which having children feels like a constraint on my freedom? How can I re-narrate that in positive terms, seeing it as an opportunity for growth?
- In what way has having children helped to make me less selfish? How can I be even more generous in embracing these necessary sacrifices?

## Do

*This Week: Examine Your Conscience*

The examination of conscience is a traditional Catholic practice wherein a person considers his or her past thoughts, words, and actions in order to recognize sin and failings. Normally, a penitent does an examination of conscience before receiving the Sacrament of Reconciliation, but it is helpful for spiritual growth to take a minute or two for a daily examination. In identifying sin in our lives, we might consider using the Ten Commandments, the Beatitudes, or a written examination of conscience, such as those found on the United States Conference of Catholic Bishops website.[†] It may also be helpful to consider our thoughts and actions from a God's-eye view. Where did we seek to do our own will rather than trying to see and live God's will?

---

[†] http://www.usccb.org/prayer-and-worship/sacraments-and-sacramentals/penance/examinations-of-conscience.cfm

# FIRST SUNDAY OF LENT, YEAR B

## *Year B (2021, 2024, 2027, 2030)*

### Read

- Genesis 9:8–15
- Psalm 25:4–5, 6–7, 8–9
  R. Your ways, O Lord, are love and truth to those who keep your covenant.
- 1 Peter 3:18–22
- Mark 1:12–15

### Reflect

On this first Sunday of Lent, we hear Mark's brief telling of Jesus' temptation by Satan in the desert and the angels ministering to Jesus. We also hear Jesus proclaiming the kingdom and calling all to repentance and belief in the Gospel. One message from this Gospel and from our other readings for the day is simple: This is our story. We are part of this narrative, and our lives thus make the most sense when we see them within a larger narrative.

It is easy to get caught up in our own lives, with all the goals, joys, and struggles. Sometimes we put ourselves at the center of a narrative that narrowly revolves around ourselves. Lent is a beautiful time to refocus, trying to look at a bigger picture and seeing our lives with a God's-eye view. Far from taking our attention off of our hopes and needs, this God's-eye perspective helps us to see our lives with greater meaning, understanding how the daily tasks of parenting are part of a larger story, rather than insignificant acts easily dismissed or forgotten.

The first reading from Genesis describes God's covenant with Noah, and the rainbow that represents God's promise never to destroy all mortal beings again. We see here, as well as in the responsorial psalm, that God truly wants what is best for us. And the second reading, from the first letter of Saint Peter, brings this out in discussing baptism, which was prefigured in those saved on Noah's ark.

In baptism, we become members of this narrative. We enter the beautiful story of God's covenant, which is completed in the life, death, and resurrection of Jesus Christ. It is given to us freely and willingly by our God, who loves us so much that he sent his only son to save us. If we are to share fully in this narrative, we must heed Jesus' call for repentance during this season of Lent. As parents, we often have to face our faults in new ways. But rather than despairing in these, we should believe in the Gospel and unite our challenges and difficulties to the cross of Christ. This is a God's-eye view of our lives as parents: God graciously gives us children to raise, and both the joys and struggles are opportunities to grow in love, repenting of our sins and believing in the Gospel.

## Pray

Remember no more the sins of my youth; remember me according to your mercy, because of your goodness, Lord. (Psalm 25:7)

## Ponder

- How does seeing your life as part of a larger narrative provide context for your life as a parent? How does it help to make sense of the most challenging parts of parenting?
- When have you become caught up in the details of life

and lost sight of God? How do you correct your course to refocus on God?

- How can you reflect on your own and your children's baptism with an eye to remembering God's covenant and your place within this larger narrative? How does it provide perspective in daily life?

## Do

*This Week: Examine Your Conscience*

The examination of conscience is a traditional Catholic practice wherein a person considers his or her past thoughts, words, and actions in order to recognize sin and failings. Normally, a penitent does an examination of conscience before receiving the Sacrament of Reconciliation, but it is helpful for spiritual growth to take a minute or two for a daily examination. In identifying sin in our lives, we might consider using the Ten Commandments, the Beatitudes, or a written examination of conscience, such as those found on the United States Conference of Catholic Bishops website.[‡] It may also be helpful to consider whether your thoughts and actions reflect a God's-eye view of your life. Ask yourself, where did I seek to do my will rather than trying to see and live God's will?

[‡] http://www.usccb.org/prayer-and-worship/sacraments-and-sacramentals/penance/examinations-of-conscience.cfm

---

# FIRST SUNDAY OF LENT, YEAR C

## *Year C (2022, 2025, 2028, 2031)*

### Read

- Deuteronomy 26:4–10
- Psalm 91:1–2, 10–11, 12–13, 14–15
  R. Be with me Lord, when I am in trouble.
- Romans 10:8–13
- Luke 4:1–13

### Reflect

As we begin this season of Lent, today's readings provide us with a certain confidence for all our endeavors during this penitential season. God is with us. It's a powerful theme carried throughout the readings. In the first reading from Deuteronomy, we hear Moses describe the affliction and oppression of the people, followed by God delivering them from Egypt. Our Gospel passage from Luke describes Jesus' temptation in the desert, and his refusals to Satan's proposals show confidence in God. The second reading reinforces this: "everyone who calls on the name of the Lord will be saved" (Rom 10:13).

During this Lent, we are invited to think about how this is our story. The Gospel passage describing Jesus' temptation in the desert contains more than it appears at a quick read. Jesus withstands the Devil's temptations, and he will continue to stay true to his course, even when it involves his passion and death. We know how this particular drama concludes: with the glory of the

Resurrection on Easter Sunday. And when we immerse ourselves in Jesus' life and death, we share in the final victory.

When we see ourselves as part of this narrative, we cultivate a God's-eye view of our lives as parents. God is always on our side, and so we live with a degree of confidence appropriate to faith and hope. At times, we may fall into the trap of limiting ourselves with a narrow view; it is easy to become lost in the moment, as did the Israelites in those long days of slavery in Egypt. In the bigger picture, we see that God was with the people then and had a plan for their freedom. When that freedom was realized in the promised land, the people could properly thank God for his guidance that was now so obvious as they looked back over their history.

As parents, we don't always see or understand the significance of the moment, especially in times of stress or difficulty. We may succumb to temptations, looking for easy ways out of the challenges we face or despairing when we encounter difficulty. The story of Lent and Easter calls us back to where we belong; we believe in Jesus with the heart and profess it with our words (see Rom 10:10). We are able and willing to put our lives in God's hands, to unite our struggles to the cross, to recognize our sins and do penance for them, and we believe that God will provide the grace we need to do his will. And when we see ourselves within this narrative of God's mercy, we can flourish in our lives as parents. It may not always be fun or feel easy, but with a God's-eye perspective, we see that it is meaningful and, ultimately, joyful.

## Pray

Everyone who calls on the name of the Lord will be saved. (Romans 10:13)

## Ponder

- How do you face your parenting struggles with confidence? How do they bring you closer to God?

- What temptations do you face in your current life? How do you look to Jesus for aid in withstanding these?
- Can you look back over your life and see God's hand guiding you? How does seeing yourself within a larger narrative of God's love and Jesus' resurrection help you to be joyful during the season of Lent?

## Do

*This Week: Examine Your Conscience*

The examination of conscience is a traditional Catholic practice wherein a person considers his or her past thoughts, words, and actions in order to recognize sin and failings. Normally, a penitent does an examination of conscience before receiving the Sacrament of Reconciliation, but it is helpful for spiritual growth to take a minute or two for a daily examination. In identifying sin in our lives, we might consider using the Ten Commandments, the Beatitudes, or a written examination of conscience, such as those found on the United States Conference of Catholic Bishops website.[§] It may also be helpful to consider whether your thoughts and actions reflect a God's-eye view of your life. Ask yourself, where did I seek to do my will rather than trying to see and live God's will?

---

§ http://www.usccb.org/prayer-and-worship/sacraments-and-sacramentals/penance/examinations-of-conscience.cfm

---

# MONDAY

## Read

- Leviticus 19:1–2, 11–18
- Psalm 19:8, 9, 10, 15
  R. Your words, Lord, are Spirit and life.
- Matthew 25:31–46

## Reflect

Our Gospel reading today from Matthew can seem to be one of those harsh, nerve-racking passages. It's a dramatic, if not frightening, image: a king sorting out the sheep and the goats, the good and the evil, and condemning the latter to eternal punishment. Regularly practicing an examination of conscience helps us to be quick to recognize all the ways we fall short in attending to the needs of others. Selfishness seems to come quite naturally, doesn't it?

On the other hand, how often do we recognize injustice in this world and wish for justice? We often see the ruthless advancing in success while honest, hard workers struggle. As the world often appears to us, there is no punishment for those who care only for pursuing their own desires at the expense of others, particularly those in need. And there also seems to be no obvious reward for those who make selfless sacrifices for others.

When we imbibe the perspective of the world, we can easily become discouraged or disheartened by our responsibilities as parents. Changing diapers, fixing meals, scheduling dental appointments, driving to soccer practice — these duties will not win us fame or honor in the eyes of the world. The limitations of parenting often draw us to find recognizable "success" in other pursuits: a career, running a marathon, writing a book. And indeed, we can glorify God in each of these if we offer our time dedicated to that work prayerfully.

Yet, what makes the duties of parenting unique is that their importance so often goes unrecognized, even by us. The corporal works of mercy — the ways we serve the physical and material needs of others — are intrinsic to raising children. We give them food when they are hungry, we give them drinks when they are thirsty, we accept them lovingly into our homes, providing clothes for them, caring for them in illness, and even visiting them in prison if necessary. We, and most of the world, generally fail to see these acts as significant, perhaps because so many people perform these tasks as expected.

When we take a God's-eye view, however, this Gospel passage should come immediately to mind. Ultimately, at the final judgment, there is recognition for generosity to others, including our own children. The reward for these duties is not likely to be something we experience on a day-to-day basis, but God is watching us, observing our sacrifices and the love with which we perform them. A supernatural perspective of our life shows us meaning beyond simply doing what we have to do when it comes to raising children. Rather, we are serving Christ himself in our family members, as well as others in need. This represents an amazing opportunity for grace.

## Pray

Whatever you did for one of these least brothers of mine, you did for me. (Matthew 25:40)

## Reflect

- How do I tend to devalue my unrecognized duties as a

parent, instead seeking the recognition of the world for other pursuits? Or how do I seek affirmation as a parent through the success of my children?

- How can a supernatural perspective of my parenting responsibilities help me to act more generously toward my children?
- In what ways can I re-narrate my frustrations in light of this Gospel passage? How can I remember the presence of God throughout the course of the day, reminding myself that he sees and appreciates the ways that I serve others?

## Do

*This Week: Examine Your Conscience*

When we do today's examination of conscience, we might find it helpful to consider the ways we have not seen Christ in others in need, including our children. Have we been generous and cheerful in responding to the needs of our children and others? Do we see Christ in them? Do we tend to seek worldly recognition in other pursuits to compensate for the lack we feel with parenting? Do we feel resentful and dissatisfied when called upon to perform corporal works of mercy?

---

# TUESDAY

## Read

- Isaiah 55:10–11
- Psalm 34:4–5, 6–7, 16–17, 18–19
  R. From all their distress God rescues the just.
- Matthew 6:7–15

## Reflect

The Our Father prayer is probably one of the prayers you have known longest in your life. There is good reason that this prayer is prioritized for Christians: It was spoken by Jesus himself as instruction for us. Yet, how often do we casually recite this prayer without even giving thought to the words?

Jesus provides this prayer as a contrast to the pagans, who babble with many words even though God knows what you need before you tell him. And here is the real struggle: We may agree or, at least, want to agree with Jesus' words. We want to believe that God knows what we need. And yet, often, especially when it comes to raising children, God doesn't give us what we think we need. Thus we may find ourselves babbling like pagans, making demands that God conform to our will. We may even come up with clever reasons or explanations for why God should do what we want.

For example, we may have a child who doesn't seem to live up to our expectations. Perhaps we expect dedication, commitment, and work ethic, and the child just appears to be lazy. We may say to ourselves that this is clearly bad; we want the child to develop the virtue of constancy. Surely God wants that too, right? Doesn't God want our children to be the best they can be? Doesn't God want our children to make the most of their gifts and talents?

These questions may distract us from truly following God's will for us and for our children. We may not understand why we encounter certain difficulties with our children; our limited human vision simply does not provide us with a big picture, God's-eye view of the situation. And when we seek to dominate every challenge, making demands of God for an immediate fix to our problems, we lose the humility expressed in the Our Father.

This prayer is about honoring God. We must seek, honor, and love God's will in our lives. This is true even if that will seems to involve obstinate, severely ill, or even gravely sinful children. We pray that our children and the challenges they present do not become occasions for our own sin; but rather, opportunities for us to depend more fully on God, seeking forgiveness for our sins, and looking to the daily bread of the Eucharist for sustenance in the midst of these challenges.

As we live this Lent, it will be easier if we acknowledge our limited vision of our family life. While our role is crucial, and our parenting requires constant reflection and discernment, there is much outside of our control. From a natural perspective, this is nothing but frustrating and discouraging. Yet, we can't predict how these situations may hold great supernatural importance. We may not even recognize the graces we received in these trials until many years later. God's ways are not our ways; and yet, his ways are always infinitely better for us than we could imagine.

## Pray

Look to him and be radiant, and your faces may not blush for shame. (Psalm 34:6)

## Ponder

- In what instances do I need to trust more in God's will,

rather than praying that God does what I want?

- How can I acknowledge my limited vision when it comes to my children's lives, and open my eyes to a God's-eye view?
- What must I do to depend more fully on Jesus? How can I grow in Eucharistic devotion? How do I recognize that salvation comes from Christ and not from myself?

## Do

*This Week: Examine Your Conscience*

As we perform today's examination of conscience, let us consider the ways we seek to force God's hand, wanting God's will to conform to ours, rather than the other way around. At what point does always wanting everything our own way become a sin of distrust in God? What challenges of parenting do we initially reject as worthless, rather than acknowledging that they may be supernaturally purposeful from a God's-eye perspective? Looking ahead to tomorrow, how can we turn our focus to God, honoring him and accepting his will in whatever might happen?

# WEDNESDAY

**Read**

- Jonah 3:1–10
- Psalm 51:3–4, 12–13, 18–19

  R. A heart contrite and humbled, O God, you will not spurn.
- Luke 11:29–32

**Reflect**

Does life with children feel like a continual Lent to you? Before children, we might have chosen a Lenten resolution that caused us to sacrifice a creature comfort such as a favorite food, activity, or beverage. After children, however, we live a life that features nonstop sacrifices of our comfort. We parents generally get less sleep, have fewer opportunities for dining out, frequently trip over toys, and must figure out how to share resources among the family, rather than simply prioritizing our own desires.

Parents can appear largely unhappy when compared with childless people! And it's no wonder, considering the numerous restrictions and stressors that come with parenting. It is easy, under these circumstances, to begin harboring some resentment. Even when we know we've undertaken this life willingly and truly are grateful for our children, we may find ourselves thinking, "All I want is to drink my morning coffee without having to be interrupted to clean up a huge mess!"

Then there are also ways that children seem bent upon sabotaging our spiritual lives. We may have treasured the beauty of Sunday Mass, and now we find ourselves confined to the vestibule for almost the entirety of the service. Perhaps we had time to attend group Rosaries and novenas, and now we don't. We were able to live a recollected life, focused on serving God in our work and leisure, and now we run around like crazy people, just trying to get everything done … but never being able to do so!

Resentment comes naturally in such situations, but it can become dangerous to feed that resentment. It can foster a sort of pride, where we feel like we deserve better. We may succumb to a problematic understanding of life, believing that we know exactly what we need for happiness and fulfillment, but we just aren't getting it. Of course, there may be times where we need to re-evaluate the stresses of parenting and find ways to alleviate certain situations or make changes to improve our lives. But there are also times when we need to ask ourselves: Where is Jesus in these struggles?

Do we recognize him as something greater than Solomon, greater than Jonah? Do we see him calling us to great sacrifices lovingly made, as he himself did? Do we believe that we can share in his strength when we share in his human weaknesses? Do we see that recognizing our sin and responding with repentance can fulfill us, rather than taking away our happiness? If we can fight the skepticism that causes us to think we know better, then we have a chance of embracing God's will even during the worst parts of parenting. We know we have sinned and continue to sin, and thus these challenges, and the sacrifices we make for them, are powerful opportunities for immediate repentance. In embracing the difficult moments as God's will, we can make reparation for our past sins, as well as strive to change our ways to reflect better our love for God and willingness to do his will, rather than ours.

From a supernatural perspective, this willingness to offer our struggles as penance for our sin aids us in cultivating a God's-eye view for our life. Hebrews 12:6 tells us that God chastises those whom he loves. In providing us with the difficulties of parenting, God is giving us a gift. God wants us to become better, happier people, and he knows the way this happens is by depending more fully on him for our happiness. We can become more free when we embrace his will and choose to offer these difficulties to him, rather than resenting and avoiding them, thinking we know better. We want to respond like the people of Nineveh, heeding the word of God, recognizing our sins, embracing our penance — both the voluntary Lenten resolutions and the involuntary daily sacrifices of parenting.

## Pray

Have mercy on me, God, in accord with your merciful love. (Psalm 51:3)

## Ponder

- How do I need to improve at recognizing my sins and seeking forgiveness? When my kids or spouse rightly point out a failing, do I contradict them resentfully or acknowledge it gratefully with an apology?
- Do I see my voluntary Lenten resolution as related to the many involuntary sacrifices that I make in my life as a parent? How can I offer both as penance for my own sins?
- How have I become resentful of the inconveniences and difficulties of parenting? Do I give in to excessive complaining? Can I try to approach the challenges with a sense of humor and greater supernatural perspective?

## Do

*This Week: Examine Your Conscience*

Today, when we are examining our consciences, let us ask ourselves how we seek to be in control and how we react when something doesn't go according to plan. Do we have the humility to recognize that God might be calling us to something else? Have we tried to see Jesus present in the midst of frustrations? Do we recognize our sins and failings quickly and immediately try to respond by acknowledging them and offering penance?

# THURSDAY

## Read

- Esther C:12, 14–16, 23–25
- Psalm 138:1–2AB, 2CDE–3, 7C–8

  R. Lord, on the day I called for help, you answered me.
- Matthew 7:7–12

## Reflect

Sometimes, in our lowest moments, we find ourselves grasping for God. These events bring out our recognition of our complete dependence on him. We know that circumstances are beyond our control. As strong-willed or hard-working as we might be, we simply aren't always in charge.

Queen Esther finds herself in such a situation in our first reading. Haman is orchestrating to kill all the Jews in the kingdom of Persia, and Esther is informed of this by Mordecai. Although she is a queen, she has limited influence in the royal court. Esther is willing to do whatever it takes to intercede with the king for their protection from Haman's decree, but she isn't certain of what she can do to intercede. Thus, she prays in desperation to God.

Perhaps we have found ourselves in situations where we fear for the life of a child or someone else we love. We may beg God to spare our child some suffering; or, in the midst of labor and delivery, we may pray fervently for the quick birth of a healthy child! There is something beautiful about how we instinctively reach out to God at these times. It shows a humility on our part, as well as hope and confidence in God. We feel our littleness and inability, and we call out the immensity and power of God, who alone can help us in our distress.

For Queen Esther, recourse to God came somewhat naturally. She was a faithful Jew, who must have called on God many times, whether in gratitude or in need. We also should cultivate this recourse to God, not just in those big, momentous difficulties, but in all the smaller moments, too. From discovering red permanent marker on the living room wall, to sharing in the joy of a child's first Communion or confirmation, we want instinctively to bring our experiences and emotions to God, seeking intimacy at all times. God desires to be with us in the big moments, but God also wants to be part of our lives in the midst of ordinary details, from choosing kids' activities to deciding what to make for dinner.

From a supernatural perspective, nothing is too insignificant for God, because we are never insignificant in his eyes. Although it can be difficult to comprehend, God loves each of us uniquely, and he wants to give us what is best for us at all times. In our roles as parents, we may often feel that we aren't really getting what we need. We might feel overwhelmed at times, and we lack perspective on the big picture because we can't know, as God does, what the future holds. Sometimes, we are only able to understand the meaning of certain events years later, and then we see the grace — how God was working in our lives.

Part of cultivating a God's-eye view is recognizing our limited vision and turning to God in our need. Whether everything turns out just as we wanted or our worst nightmares come true, we must depend on God with the confidence of children. We have been given salvation through Jesus' life, death, and resurrection. This gift goes beyond God's saving the Jewish people during Esther's time; it continues to bring meaning and hope to us during our darkest times.

## Pray

On the day I cried out, you answered. (Psalm 138:3A)

## Ponder

- When was a time of great need where I found myself calling out to God in desperation? Did this deepen my relationship with God when the situation was over?
- How do I try to cultivate a habit of needing God, involving him in the ordinary details and frustrations of life? How can I improve in this area?
- Do I practice persistence in prayer? Do I trust that God is our loving, heavenly father who will give me all I need?

## Do

*This Week: Examine Your Conscience*

As we review our day, let us ask where we fail to incorporate God into our daily life and tasks. Do we try to do everything on our own? How have we not had recourse to God in times of trouble (both large and small)? Do we seek God's support in struggling against our own sins and failings?

---

# FRIDAY

## Read

- Ezekiel 18:21–28
- Psalm 130:1–2, 3–4, 5–7A, 7BC–8
  R. If you, O Lord, mark iniquities, who can stand?
- Matthew 5:20–26

## Reflect

"The LORD's way is not fair!" How often do we say or think these words from Ezekiel 18:25? Particularly in those times where we undergo struggle or disappointment, we are apt to blame God rather than accept his way. When a loved one suddenly becomes grievously ill or dies in a sudden accident, we cry, "It's not fair!" In today's first reading, however, the unfairness of the Lord is shown in the way he forgives the wicked who turn from evil to virtue while punishing those who, once virtuous, now pursue evil.

How unlike God are we in this regard! We hold grudges and are hesitant to forgive, especially when we have suffered from someone else's sins. It doesn't seem fair to us that someone can wound others by bad behavior and then be reconciled to God and saved. We prefer that sinners "get what was coming to them," as a result of their actions.

God always wants what is best for sinners, and that includes us, too! God wants our repentance, and God won't hold our sins against us, demanding reparation indefinitely. It is hard to understand God's mercy, because he doesn't follow our conventional ideas of justice. We can never adequately pay God back for the sins we commit against him, but he will always accept a truly contrite heart seeking to make amends. His mercy is not contrary to human justice, but rather beyond human justice.

Although we may find it hard to understand, and we might not like knowing that others have repented and been forgiven by God, we cannot begrudge this. After all, we too are beneficiaries of God's mercy. In our stubbornness, we may feel his forgiveness unnecessary and unwanted, or we may feel undeserving of God's mercy. As parents, we sometimes are painfully aware of our failures. When we see the negative effects that our selfishness and mistakes have had on our children, we might hold grudges against ourselves, believing that we cannot move beyond such weaknesses and sins.

This, however, is not the Lord's way. God does not seek to punish indefinitely, cutting his children off from his love. Rather, he always invites us back and wants us back, like the father of the prodigal son (see Lk 15:11–32). God wants what is best for us: namely, himself. The implication of this supernatural view is powerful, for even the absolute worst moments of our parenting can bring us closer to God. When we recognize the Lord's way, we see that our mistakes and sins provide an opportunity to humble ourselves, admitting our weakness and dependence on God. If we consistently turn back to God, we will grow in virtue as well as love for God and God's way.

## Pray

With the LORD is mercy. (Psalm 130:7BC)

## Ponder

- Where do I tend toward judgment and criticism of those around me? When have I held a grudge and even desired ill toward a person who had wronged me?
- When have I extended mercy and forgiveness to my

children? Have I demonstrated an ability to accept their apologies and continue without resentment or anger toward them?

- How does God's mercy transcend the justice I deserve? When have I felt his forgiveness come to me undeserved? And how can I also forgive myself when God has forgiven me, rather than holding on to resentment against myself?

**Do**

*This Week: Examine Your Conscience*

We see how quickly and easily the Lord forgives those who turn away from evil and sin. But to do this "turning away," this repentance, requires recognition and acknowledgment of the sins and desire and will to do otherwise. Hence we can see just how important the examination of conscience is for our repentance during this season of Lent. God's mercy is readily available to us when we admit our sin. Today we take some time to identify our sins and ask not only for forgiveness, but also for the strength to recommit ourselves to virtue.

# SATURDAY

## Read

- Deuteronomy 26:16–19
- Psalm 119:1–2, 4–5, 7–8
  R. Blessed are they who follow the law of the Lord!
- Matthew 5:43–48

## Reflect

In recent years, we have heard that the legalism of the Church (and perhaps of God) is a problem. If we only follow the law, we fall short of the love we are called to exhibit. We can become too worried about all the details of rigidly adhering to the prescribed laws. In our first reading, however, we hear a different perspective on law. As today's psalm says, "Blessed those whose way is blameless, who walk by the law of the LORD" (Ps 119:1a). Rather than pitting the law against love, we seem to hear that following God's law is a way of showing love to God.

Think about some of the rules we put in place for our children. For example, perhaps we are keen to limit their screen time, per the advice of professionals who suggest too much time watching TV or interacting with a tablet has adverse effects on children. From the child's perspective, we are simply limiting their fun, imposing a rule that they don't like. When we enforce our rules in this area, our children react with frustration and even anger. But we know that these rules have our children's best interests at heart; they are designed to increase their freedom rather than restrict it. And although we dislike being the target of their frustrations, we don't feel any better if we decide not to enforce the rules, for then we feel that we are failing them.

Likewise, God's laws facilitate our freedom, rather than restrict it. When we feel affection for God and a desire to please him, we are more apt to embrace his laws, recognizing that, as a loving father, he has established them for our benefit. In Deuteronomy, Moses describes the law as an agreement between the people and God. The people will observe God's laws, walking in his way and heeding his voice; and meanwhile, the people will be sacred to the Lord, a people peculiarly his own.

With Jesus, our Lord and Savior and brother, coming among us as a human, this is more true than ever. We are not only a people of God, but children of God, as Jesus himself mentions in today's Gospel passage. The fact is that, like the people of Israel, we haven't always followed God's law as we intended. But despite that, the Lord has remained faithful to us, and Jesus has come to our aid, offering himself to make up for all the ways we have failed. Our freedom is facilitated by following the law of God; but, to the extent that we fail, our freedom is facilitated by our humility in turning to Christ, acknowledging our sin and desiring that he make up for all that is lacking within us.

In our role as parents, we try hard to do our best because we know that it is also what is best for our children. Parenting with love is also what is best for us; we become better and holier people as we improve at making daily sacrifices without resentment. It is not always easy; but, like striving to follow God's law, we show our love and commitment to God when we make the effort.

## Pray

Blessed those who keep his testimonies, who seek him with all their heart. (Psalm 119:2)

## Ponder

- What Church rules do I feel are restrictions on my freedom? How might I re-narrate these rules, understanding them as God's loving invitation to freedom?
- What is an example of a rule I have imposed on my children in their best interest? How do I convey to them that this rule is meant to guide and help them? How do I comfort them, acknowledging their frustrations at having to follow household rules?
- What is the significance of being children of God? How does Jesus come to my aid when I have failed to follow God's laws out of love?

## Do

*This Week: Examine Your Conscience*

For years, examinations of conscience have been based on the Ten Commandments found in the Old Testament. To many of us, these rules, such as "Thou shalt not kill," fall short of a helpful guide, focusing narrowly on these ancient laws of God. However, when we recognize the complexity and extent of the rules, including our anger that seeks to wound someone, we can see that these rules can be truly helpful. As we examine our consciences today, we ask ourselves how we can recognize and reject the times we've failed to love God by not following his laws and not wanting to do his will. Then, let us ask him to show us how to grow closer to him despite our faults.

# SECOND WEEK OF LENT

## *Letting Go of Control*

# SECOND SUNDAY OF LENT, YEAR A

## Read

- Genesis 12:1–4A
- Psalm 33:4–5, 18–19, 20, 22
  R. Lord, let your mercy be on us, as we place our trust in you.
- 2 Timothy 1:8B–10
- Matthew 17:1–9

## Reflect

Wanting to be in control seems to be simply part of the human condition. Perhaps we can attribute that to the gift of free will; we know we are capable of making decisions in our minds and carrying them out with our actions. Our choices are important and crucial to who we are and aspire to be. And yet, we must also admit that our plans don't always work out as we wanted, and we often find our choices limited in ways we cannot control. This is particularly true when we have children! Suddenly, we find ourselves constantly reacting to someone else, rather than making decisions on our own.

For this second week of Lent, we will focus on letting go of control, while embracing detachment and humility. You probably already realize that parenting is not an area in which you can ever have complete control. That means an uncomfortable detachment from our own ideas and plans, as well as humility to acknowledge that what we receive in life can actually be better for us as persons on a journey to God.

Today's first reading is a great example of trusting in God. Abram, later known as Abraham, has every reason to doubt what God describes as his future. God tells Abram that he will make of him a great nation, but Abram knows that he and his wife, Sarai, are infertile and aged. They are settled and comfortable; but when God tells him to leave his homeland, Abram goes, just as the Lord directed. He exhibits trust, born of detachment and humility.

Sometimes we become so wrapped up in our own ideas, and discouraged by our disappointments, that we are paralyzed in our pride. We don't believe that even our sufferings might be part of God's plan for redemption. We would rather wallow in sorrow and become set in our ways than follow the new direction to which God calls us, especially if that means leaving behind comfort and stability.

In the second reading, from Saint Paul's second letter to Timothy, we hear a call to "Bear your share of hardship for the Gospel with the strength that comes from God" (2 Tm 1:8B). Paul emphasizes that we are called to a holy life, according to God's own design, rather than our own works. This is because God loves us and knows what is best for us! There will be hard times, but when we love God and recognize his love for us, we will have the strength we need to live our best lives. A key in these first two readings, and the psalm, is the emphasis to trust in God, which means letting go of control and letting God be in charge, no matter what.

Of course, that's not the end of the story. If the Christian Faith — or the season of Lent — were merely about suffering, it wouldn't be compelling to so many. Rather, we have a hope that the suffering and hardship are ultimately meaningful for us, and we find that hope in the Gospel passage depicting Jesus' Transfiguration. The disciples on the mountain with Jesus witness him transformed in glory, a vision of his resurrection.

In the midst of these long days of Lent, this is our vision as well. Abram left the security of his homeland out of hope for the future and trust in God's plan for his life, and ultimately ended up being the father of the whole Jewish people. Saint Paul reminds us that we share not only in Jesus' suffering, but also in his victory over death. As we begin this second full week of Lent, let us keep all this in mind. We are pilgrim people on a journey that will involve suffering and hardship, but we live in the hope of redemption through Jesus Christ.

## Pray

May your mercy, LORD, be upon us. (Psalm 33:22)

## Ponder

- In what ways to do I seek complete control in my parental duties and family life? How does that frustrate me, and inhibit my trust in God?
- Where have my expectations for parenting turned out to be difficult to fulfill, or even just mistaken? How has that helped me to grow as a person and child of God?
- How can I better unite my hardships and sufferings to Christ's cross, with the hope of sharing in his glory of the Resurrection?

## Do

*This Week: Fasting*

Fasting can take many different forms, and Lenten resolutions often involve a fast of some sort, from sweets or meat or something to which you are particularly or unhealthily attached. If we have already chosen this sort of resolution, we can take this week to focus on that sacrifice more prayerfully. Otherwise, if we are able to do so, let us consider not eating between meals this week, with the goal of detaching from control and attaching ourselves more fully in humility to God.

# SECOND SUNDAY OF LENT, YEAR B

## Read

- Genesis 22:1–2, 9A, 10–13, 15–18
- Psalm 116:10, 15, 16–17, 18–19
  R. I will walk before the Lord, in the land of the living.
- Romans 8:31B–34
- Mark 9:2–10

## Reflect

For parents, the story of Abraham called to sacrifice his son Isaac can be tough. We can easily place ourselves in Abraham's position, knowing the love we have for our child and our hopes for that child's future. Would we assent to God's request as Abraham did? Can we imagine being willing to do what God asked, even when it involved this kind of sacrifice?

Abraham demonstrates great trust in God in this story. He was willing to relinquish his own desires and hopes for his child; he let go of control. And, of course, what we see in this story is that ultimately, Abraham does not have to kill his son. Abraham's seeking to do God's will instead of acting on his own preferences is rewarded abundantly by God. Isaac lives, and through him Abraham becomes the father of a great nation.

But that isn't the end of the story. The account of Abraham not sacrificing his son is paired with a Gospel reading from Mark describing Jesus' Transfiguration, where he is identified as the Son of God. And while Isaac is spared from death, Jesus is not.

The Transfiguration, witnessed by Peter, James, and John, is a prefiguring of the Resurrection, and Jesus tells these three not to mention his Transfiguration until "the Son of Man had risen from the dead" (Mk 9:9).

So many times as parents, we want to be in control. Admittedly, we have many responsibilities that depend upon our choices, from deciding kids' activities to choosing what's for dinner. Yet we simply can't be in control of everything, and the many surprises and challenges of family life can be discouraging and difficult precisely because we recognize in them our inability to have complete control. Perhaps this is why today's second reading is so encouraging, keeping us from despair: "If God is for us, who can be against us?" (Rom 8:31B).

Sometimes God's plans for our family — like his plans for Abraham's — are far beyond what we can imagine. When we make our own plans and rely upon them as though we are independent from God, we risk limiting the abundance we might receive when we seek to live according to his design. When we, like Abraham, are willing to let go of control, making sacrifices and bearing hardships, we find that God provides for us abundantly. God did not spare his own son, Jesus, who lived, suffered, died, and rose again. And so, "how will he not also give us everything else along with him?" (Rom 8:32). In letting go of control, we become able to share in Jesus' final victory over death, prefigured in the Transfiguration and revealed in the Resurrection. With the challenges we face, we see that this confidence that God is for us ultimately brings us comfort and peace.

### Pray

I will offer a sacrifice of praise and call on the name of the LORD. (Psalm 116:17)

## Ponder

- What sacrifices has the Lord asked me to make as a parent? How can I embrace them willingly and with confidence in God's abundance?
- Have there been any incidents in my life that reminded me of my lack of control? How did I handle them?
- How can I remember that God is for me and my family in times of difficulty? When have I felt God's grace and abundance in my family life?

## Do

*This Week: Fasting*

Fasting can take many different forms, and Lenten resolutions often involve a fast of some sort, from sweets or meat or something to which you are particularly or unhealthily attached. If we have already chosen this sort of resolution, we can take this week to focus on that sacrifice more prayerfully. Otherwise, if we are able to do so, let us consider not eating between meals this week, with the goal of detaching from control and attaching ourselves more fully in humility to God.

# SECOND SUNDAY OF LENT, YEAR C

## Read

- Genesis 15:5–12, 17–18
- Psalm 27:1, 7–8, 8–9, 13–14
  R. The Lord is my light and my salvation.
- Philippians 3:17—4:1
- Luke 9:28B–36

## Reflect

During the season of Lent — and indeed, even in our ordinary lives as parents — it can become easy to get bogged down in difficulties and challenges. Today's readings, however, remind us that we are called to, and belong to, something greater than our current circumstances might indicate. In the Gospel reading from Luke, we hear the story of Jesus' Transfiguration on the mountaintop, which prefigures his resurrection from the dead. This passage helps us to keep our eyes focused not simply on Lent, but rather on what comes after Lent: Jesus' resurrection from the dead, which we particularly celebrate on Easter.

As parents, we have many responsibilities. We are in charge of much in the day-to-day running of a household and the choices we make with respect to our children, from their education to their nutrition. We feel the need to be in control; and yet, there are so many moments when we realize that we don't truly have control. Sometimes a child doesn't get into the college of her choice, or a toddler writes all over the wall with a permanent marker.

Although such moments are beyond our control, they are

also amazing opportunities to remind ourselves of all that lies ahead of us. In this life on earth, we will encounter struggle, but we can't let the misfortunes or even the mundane tasks of daily life distract us from the knowledge that we are citizens of heaven, as the second reading states (Phil 3:20). We stand firm in the Lord, knowing all that lies in store for us.

When we let go of wanting our own expectations to win out and our own will to dominate, then we open ourselves to the grace of God, who is always ultimately in charge of our lives. Just as God provided abundantly for Abraham and his family, God will provide abundantly for us.

## Pray

The Lord is my light and my salvation. (Psalm 27:1A)

## Ponder

- When have I become bogged down in the difficulties and challenges of parenting? How did I seek to redirect my attention to God's abundance in providing for me?
- What responsibilities seem to overwhelm me? How can I place these in God's hands, keeping in mind the Resurrection that follows the cross?
- How does the knowledge of my citizenship in heaven affect the choices I make in regard to my children? How does my life as a parent exhibit trust in God?

## Do

*This Week: Fasting*

Fasting can take many different forms, and Lenten resolutions often involve a fast of some sort, from sweets or meat or something to which you are particularly or unhealthily attached. If we have already chosen this sort of resolution, we can take this week to focus on that sacrifice more prayerfully. Otherwise, if we are able to do so, let us consider not eating between meals this week, with the goal of detaching from control and attaching ourselves more fully in humility to God.

# MONDAY

**Read**

- Daniel 9:4B–10
- Psalm 79:8, 9, 11, and 13

  R. Lord, do not deal with us according to our sins.
- Luke 6:36–38

**Reflect**

We realize that this season of Lent is a season of repentance, and therefore a time of identifying and acknowledging our sins. This does not come naturally to most of us. Rather, we are reluctant to admit fault, even when confronted directly by someone whom we have hurt or offended. And yet, despite such a tendency to ignore our own sins, we often are quick to judge or criticize others. Our relationships with our spouse or children often bring out this weakness in a new way, making obvious something that might have been hidden.

It can be so painful when we finally comprehend how we have hurt someone; for example when we notice a spouse responding defensively, ready for another criticism; or when a child bursts into tears, responding to yet another angry lecture. Unsurprisingly, we can begin to despair. So much seems to be against us. We might feel a lack of support from extended family or the larger culture that doesn't value children and families. Or we may find ourselves often short on sleep from infants and toddlers who wake up during the night, or teens who come home late. We could be overwhelmed with the responsibilities of running a household or trying to work outside the home while still being present for our family.

Some days everything seems to be against us and our attempt to live a good, holy life. It's no wonder that we turn to frustration and criticism, a sort of hopelessness in such a challenging situation, where we feel we must defend ourselves — and yes, even our sins — by constantly explaining our stress and the factors that diminish our capability for being responsible.

And yet, such a prideful response does not help those around us, and we most certainly do not help ourselves. We can injure ourselves in our own self-criticism, and then turn that criticism on others. Rather, what we need is presented in today's readings: an eagerness to admit fault, to beg God's forgiveness, to recognize God's generosity, and also to give generously. With the gift of our free will, we will make mistakes and sin against God. This presents an amazing opportunity for humbling ourselves, admitting fault and confessing sins, looking to the grace of God to heal us. We want to be the kinds of parents who are calm and consistently make good choices. But God may be asking us to grow through something else: our failures.

These failures, and God's generosity in the willing forgiveness of our sins, reminds us that we are children of God. God has mercy on us in our weakness, like an understanding father who knows the struggles of his children and has compassion on them when they fail. God wants to give us every good thing, to welcome us back to his loving embrace. Our stubbornness is the only stumbling block preventing us from stepping into that grace.

The better that we become at acknowledging our sins and asking God's forgiveness, the more we can become merciful as our Father is merciful. We can and will succeed with Jesus' commands to not judge or condemn, but rather to forgive and give generously. It takes detachment from our tendency to believe that we are always right and someone else is at fault. And it takes humility to acknowledge that a situation that seems a setup for failure might actually allow us to flourish. When we try to live generously, we put ourselves in a position to recognize and receive all the gifts God wants to give us: both the joys of family life, and our own weaknesses that open us to his mercy.

## Pray

But to the Lord, our God, belong compassion and forgiveness, though we rebelled against him. (Daniel 9:9)

## Ponder

- When was an instance where I allowed myself to begin a downward spiral, rather than seeking God's forgiveness and grace at the first opportunity? What were the costs to myself and others?
- How can I build a habit of responding to my sins by asking God and others to forgive me?
- How do I sometimes see my situation as working against my attempts to grow in holiness? Where do I recognize God's generosity in the joys and struggles of parenting?

## Do

*This Week: Fasting*

One of the struggles with fasting is that it often doesn't feel meaningful or purposeful. At times, we even seek a natural benefit such as health or weight loss, rather than a spiritual benefit. Today, we can take the occasion of hunger or desire for something we're not consuming and let it be a reminder of the hunger for God's forgiveness and mercy. We might try repeating today's one-line prayer every time we feel a pang of hunger or the desire to get up and look in the fridge.

---

# TUESDAY

## Read

- Isaiah 1:10, 16–20
- Psalm 50:8–9, 16BC–17, 21, and 23
  R. To the upright I will show the saving power of God.
- Matthew 23:1–12

## Reflect

In today's Gospel passage from Matthew, Jesus tells us that "Whoever exalts himself will be humbled; but whoever humbles himself will be exalted" (Mt 23:12). This is obviously a call to humility, but how are we supposed to live humility on a daily basis? Jesus describes what does not qualify as humility: attempts to get the attention of others, seeking affirmation and honor for one's holiness, while making demands on others without offering help.

This passage is often taken as a call to hide our faith. It is so easy to be hypocritical; few of us ever attain the standards we want to uphold. And our children are often the first to notice when we don't practice what we preach! Wouldn't it be better not even to admit to our faith, lest people see and note our failures, using them as an avenue to criticize the Church? Yet, Jesus isn't saying that hiding or giving up the faith is true humility, either.

Humility does not allow for hypocrisy, because it brings with it the constant awareness of one's sin and failings, as well as the desire for God's forgiveness. Our children might be right: We do fail to practice what we preach! But if we also realize this, and apologize for it, and confess it to God, we are not hypocrites who merely seek attention and affirmation for our own holiness, with little regard for the salvation of those around us.

Sometimes, our motivation to live good lives and to be good parents is only to be spared the judgment and criticism of those around us. We may even narrate this in a positive way relative to the faith; we want our family life to witness to the love of Christ. We want to look like we have it all together as perfect parents with perfect children so that people will be convinced of the Catholic way of life. And yet, the superficial appearance of happiness and holiness that seeks attention and affirmation is not an adequate representation of Christ's love or the Catholic Church. Rather, it brings with it a self-assurance and pride that is the opposite of the humility Jesus mentions. We are already exalting ourselves! Our focus should be on loving God and showing God our love by trying to do his will, rather than on how we appear to others. Even the desire to model for our children can work against us, if it stands in the place of the desire to love and serve God.

The embarrassment of responding angrily to a child in public or the mortification of a badly misbehaving child at Sunday Mass might be exactly what we need to grow in humility. Our humble acceptance, and cheerfully moving on rather than despairing or dwelling on our failures, might serve as a much more powerful witness to Christ's love than the appearance of perfection does. This is the gift of letting go of control. When we accept the moments when we aren't that example of a perfect Catholic parent, we gain a detachment from our pride that allows us to embrace a better motivation than appearance and affirmation; namely, loving and serving God. Instead of hiding our faults from others and denying them to our children, we can admit our weaknesses and make amends for our sins, living not as hypocrites, but rather, constantly improving children of God.

**Pray**

Whoever humbles himself will be exalted. (Matthew 23:12)

## Ponder

- When have I been hypocritical, not practicing what I preach or believe? Did I acknowledge this and confess it humbly, or did I fail to address the issue?
- Have I ever allowed my parenting to be guided by the fear of judgment and criticism of others? How can I amend this, recognizing my failing as a parent and offering it to God?
- Has there been an instance when I felt publicly humiliated by my children or my poor decisions as a parent? How did I grow from that situation?

## Do

*This Week: Fasting*

The readings today can bring with them a pang of guilt. We know that we often are hypocritical, seeking attention and affirmation, rather than doing works for the love of God. Fasting, which is so rare today, can often be interpreted as hypocritical, something done for show. And when we attempt to fast, it can become a source of pride, rather than humility. Today, as we fast in whatever way we have chosen, keep in mind that this fast is not about our own self-control and amazing spiritual ability, but rather the generous gift of God, who loves us and desires our love.

---

# WEDNESDAY

## Read

- Jeremiah 18:18–20
- Psalm 31:5–6, 14, 15–16
  R. Save me, O Lord, in your kindness.
- Matthew 20:17–28

## Reflect

Today's Gospel passage shows us the mother of the sons of Zebedee putting herself forward with a request for her sons to share in Jesus' reign. Jesus' answer may seem elusive to her, but Jesus uses his answer to foretell what it means for him to reign in his kingdom. Jesus' reign is from the cross, for it is through this suffering and death that he will be resurrected. James and John will, as disciples, ultimately suffer and die as martyrs for Christ; so in a sense, they are sharing in his chalice. They can't really know all that at this point, however. And it is clearly only a share in the glory of Jesus that their mother wants to secure.

How often do we want to jump to the happy conclusion without going through the difficulty and suffering that is necessary? How frequently do we want all the joys without the challenges? With parenting, we find many consolations, from our children's daily growth in learning and maturity to sharing with them as they receive the sacraments. Many of these little joys we eagerly anticipated even before the birth of our children.

Like the mother of James and John, we see all the potential in our children for success. We love them with a unique and passionate love. They are our children, whom we believe are deserving of every good gift. It's no surprise if we find ourselves wanting them to be celebrated and identified as special, gifted, important. And hopefully, like the mother of James and John, we want them to be close to Jesus and recognized as friends of Jesus.

Yet, as much as we desire their happiness and success, as well as their closeness to Jesus, we must heed these words of Christ. The ultimate sharing in the glory of Christ is found on the cross. We, and our children, reign with Jesus to the extent that we follow his example. And this means embracing the suffering and difficulties, rather than shunning them for success and honor as the world defines it.

Jesus tells us in today's Gospel that the one who wants to be the greatest must be the least; the one who wants to be first must be the slave of others. Jesus is our model in this; he "did not come to be served but to serve and to give his life as a ransom for many" (Mt 20:28). This humility is a hallmark of the Christian life, and, particularly in this season of Lent, we should examine how we attempt to live humility in our own lives as people, and as parents.

## Pray

Free me from the net they have set for me, for you are my refuge. (Psalm 31:5)

## Ponder

- How do I desire the success of my children? What goals do I have for them?
- Do I tend toward a focus on the earthly goals prioritized by our society? Do I keep in mind that the ultimate goal, for myself and my children, is eternal life in heaven?
- Do I ever acknowledge that my plans for my children might be different from God's plans for them? How do I let go of control and become detached from my own plans?

**Do**

*This Week: Fasting*

Our first reading and psalm depict people calling out to God in the midst of great trial, and in the Gospel reading, Jesus reminds his disciples that the greatest in the kingdom will be those who serve. Today in our fasting, we can use the desire for food or drink as an occasion to call out for God's kindness. Every discomfort can be an opportunity to think of ourselves as humble servants, letting go of our own control and calling out for the help of God our Father.

---

# THURSDAY

## Read

- Jeremiah 17:5–10
- Psalm 1:1–2, 3, 4, and 6

  R. Blessed are they who hope in the Lord.
- Luke 16:19–31

## Reflect

We are born into this world in the midst of other human beings, and our relationships with these people — family, friends, acquaintances — affect us deeply. One of our responsibilities as parents is to try to foster a loving family environment that is a comfort, and even a sanctuary, where our children feel safe and valued.

And yet, we are also called beyond these human relationships to something even more significant that ought to define our life. Today's psalm response says, "Blessed are they who hope in the Lord." This hope in the Lord, as well as faith in God and the love of God, must guide us in all our actions, including the relationships we form with others, even our family members. For if we can see God in others and recognize Christ present in them, we can also see where they are lacking and can never ultimately complete or fulfill us by themselves. We are made for God, and nothing else will suffice.

In today's Gospel from Luke, Jesus shares a parable with the Pharisees. The story can be understood simply as showing how the wealthy, who enjoyed life on earth, will suffer the torment of hell after death, whereas the poor who suffered will be rewarded in heaven. And, indeed, we must keep this bigger picture of eternal life in mind when we pursue the comforts and joys of earthly life while avoiding suffering and rejecting difficulty. We believe in life after death, and that life is forever, hence much more significant than what we enjoy or endure here on earth.

However, there is also more to this story. For we see that the wealthy man still cares for his family and desires salvation for them, even as he undergoes torment. To his pleas for help, Abraham suggests listening to Moses and the prophets, but the wealthy man insists that someone coming from the dead would be more convincing. As Jesus tells the story, Abraham concludes, saying: "If they will not listen to Moses and the prophets, neither will they be persuaded if someone should rise from the dead" (Lk 16:31). This, of course, hints at Jesus' resurrection, connecting it with the larger tradition of the Old Testament.

The Pharisees believe in resurrection, but will they accept Jesus' resurrection? Can they hope in God when they put so much emphasis on human relationships and practices? If they truly desire what is best for others, they must relinquish the control that they seek, detaching from their own ideas and convictions, and instead seeking to trust in God above all else. We must do the same, and that requires humility, a willingness to acknowledge our own ignorance when it comes to the will of God.

Like the Pharisees, we are prevented from hearing the words of the prophets, Moses, and Jesus when we trust in human relationships above all else. No matter how profound or comforting, these relationships do not bring us salvation. Jesus' resurrection is where we are saved, but before this resurrection, we find the suffering of the cross.

Our very lives as parents seem to revolve around other people — the spouse we chose and the children we are raising. Yet, we also recognize that our lives truly revolve around God, and our relationship with Christ guides and directs all of our other relationships. As we live this season of Lent, we strive to deepen that relationship by increasing our trust in God, letting go of our own control, detaching from our plans, and seeking to do his will.

**Pray**

Jesus, I trust in you.

**Ponder**

- When have I thought I understood someone and trusted in a human relationship, only to find disappointment and misunderstanding?
- How do I maintain humility when it comes to understanding my children? Do I ever find it frustrating to try to understand how they are making their decisions?
- Where do I need to relinquish control when it comes to raising my children? How could acknowledging my own ignorance and ability to control their futures help both me and them?

**Do**

*This Week: Fasting*

Today's parable contrasting the wealthy man who dined sumptuously with the poor man Lazarus should remind us of the passing value of the comforts of food on earth. The pangs of hunger or difficulty of sacrifice recall the more important comfort that we seek, that of eternal life with Christ. Today, as we continue whatever we have chosen as a fasting practice, we can recall this story of Lazarus and remind ourselves that often hunger brings us closer to God than comfort.

# FRIDAY

## Read

- Genesis 37:3–4, 12–13A, 17B–28A
- Psalm 105:16–17, 18–19, 20–21
  R. Remember the marvels the Lord has done.
- Matthew 21:33–43, 45–46

## Reflect

We are part of a much larger narrative than simply that of our own lives or that of our family. Of course, we rightly understand ourselves as the lead character in our individual story, and we have an important role in determining how our story will play out. We make decisions and react to events in important ways. And yet, we are part of a much bigger story as well. While our role is certainly crucial to us, since we are the main character, in the larger narrative shared by many we have not the significance of Joseph in this first reading, or of Jesus as he tells this parable in the Gospel passage.

During this second week of Lent, we have been reflecting on letting go of control. Detachment and humility are crucial to this task of relinquishing our desire to be in charge. And one gift of knowing and appreciating the larger narratives, including the stories found in the readings for today, is that we recognize our own littleness in comparison. We are faced with a paradox. We are uniquely loved and appreciated by God, and our life is a gift to us that we must try to offer back to God. And yet, we are also one of many who are so loved and appreciated by God. We are thus the most important, as well as insignificant when we consider the larger story of salvation, in which Jesus will always be the only true hero. The saints and angels and all who appear heroic are only so to the extent that they share in the life, death, and resurrection of Christ.

And so it is also with us. We cannot save ourselves, and no amount of fierce dedication and commitment to fulfilling our own plans will bring our salvation. This point was difficult for the chief priests and elders to understand. Jesus addresses the parable of the vineyard owner to them, and we see in this story a willful disregard for the landowner, as the tenants grasp at the produce of the harvest, seeking it for themselves when it clearly belongs to the landowner. The servants who represent the landowner are similarly treated with disrespect, and here we see an allusion to the prophets who sought to correct the people and call them back to their duties given by God.

The tenants continue to seek the fruits of the land for themselves, protecting their unjust claims through violence, even when sent the son of the landowner. Here Jesus makes an allusion to himself. God is the landowner, and he has now sent his Son to the earth to obtain the produce of his vineyard. Jesus, the Son of God, foretells his own rejection and death at the hands of those who have a responsibility to serve God as his chosen people.

Our unique stories are part of this parable as well, and we take various roles in this story. We are often like the tenants, who seek to collect the fruits of the vineyard for ourselves, rather than acknowledging that all comes from and belongs to God. We sometimes regard Jesus as competition, rather than as our brother and Savior. But, to the extent that we share the suffering of the Son and embrace injustice thrust upon us, we also share in that final justice of the Resurrection. When we reframe the gift of our life in reference to a sharing in the life, death, and resurrection of Christ, we relinquish our own plans and preferences in order to become a part of the paschal mystery. Our detachment from selfishness allows us to grow in the humility and generosity necessary for living as a child of God, invited into this narrative, as are all of the children of God.

Parenting requires so much decision-making and involves so much responsibility. We will find it hard to slip away to mere supporting roles in the life of our family, even if we acknowledge our own insignificance in the larger narrative. And yet, as we approach our many decisions in guiding family life, we benefit from keeping in mind this larger picture. In some ways, it eases the burden to see that our children's futures are beyond our control. The events of the past, present, and future in our family lives are all tied up in a larger narrative where Jesus can and will save us. We are called only to do our best, responding to God's grace, and seeking to do his will at every moment.

## Pray

God himself will set me free from the hunter's snare.

## Ponder

- How can I narrate my life as part of a larger story in which Christ is the hero? How does this perspective change the pressure I feel about getting everything right within my family?
- When do I tend to overthink choices and over-discern certain decisions? How can I approach these choices and decisions with more peace and trust in God?
- Do I take care to guard against favoritism in the family? How might I improve at expressing individual love and concern for each of my children?

## Do

*This Week: Fasting*

Fridays are a special day of penance in the Church, and during this season of Lent, Fridays are days of obligatory abstinence from meat. Today, as we fast and abstain, let us be called to a larger narrative, uniting ourselves to Jesus in his own fasting, as well as the many other Catholics throughout history and around the globe who also have traditionally observed Friday as a day of penance. Remember that this is a practice that we do together.

# SATURDAY

**Read**

- Micah 7:14–15, 18–20
- Psalm 103:1–2, 3–4, 9–10, 11–12
  R. The Lord is kind and merciful.
- Luke 15:1–3, 11–32

**Reflect**

As this second week of Lent comes to an end, our theme of letting go of control appears vividly in today's readings. The whole idea of letting go of control is firmly rooted in the understanding of who God is. Today's readings give us the image of God as a shepherd and as a generous and forgiving father, one who is kind and merciful.

If we have any desire at all to be good parents, then undoubtedly we must constantly be recognizing our faults and striving to do better. And while this knowledge and these efforts are crucial to our growth as children of God, perhaps even more important is the continued recognition that God is God, and we are not. Satan was an angel who rejected that identity and sought to compete with God, to grasp at a position that was not his and belonged to God alone. And again, in the story of the fall of Adam and Eve, we see a neglect of responsibility and a desire to make decisions aside from the counsel of God, implying a disregard for God as God. In our personal sins, great and small, we also have this tendency to want absolute control — to have everything our way.

But, of course, we can't. Parenting is perhaps the ultimate lesson in this. We don't choose precisely when a child is conceived or what that child will be like as an infant or teen. It is beneficial, early on, to recognize this limit to our control and our role in fostering independence in our children. Yet, these intentions must be coupled with the firm belief in God as God. In our humility, we must recognize that God is the master author, and we play but a small role in a larger narrative. We cannot afford to forfeit this role, but neither can we seek to be the ultimate author. Thus, when we are beset by challenges and difficulties, we must avoid despair and, instead, renew our hope. Though it is frustrating not to know the larger story or be assured of a happy conclusion, we can at least rest in this: God, as God, can make good come from the worst of situations. We see this in the unjust crucifixion of Jesus followed by his resurrection.

Our first reading from Micah should be reassuring to us. We hear that God wants to and even enjoys removing the sins of his people. God responds to the betrayal of sin with his own faithfulness. The depiction of the father in Jesus' parable from the Gospel of Luke provides a similar portrayal: The father eagerly and joyfully accepts back the wasteful son who squandered his inheritance.

In this season of Lent, we focus upon our own sinfulness. This focus does not turn us to despair, but rather, turns our attention more joyfully to the mercy of God. Yes, we acknowledge, name, and do penance for our sins. We do this all, however, in a spirit of hope and trust, knowing that God is God and we are not. We let go of control because we know that he is in control. This faith makes possible our detachment from our own plans and designs for us and our children. Furthermore, if we believe that God can forgive our sins, we can also believe that he will forgive the sins of our children. Watching children fall into sin can be painful and so discouraging for a parent. Once again, our reassurance comes from knowing God will want to forgive our children and will faithfully continue to seek them out, even when we cannot recognize his grace working in their lives.

## Pray

Merciful and gracious is the Lord, slow to anger, abounding in mercy. (Psalm 103:8A)

## Ponder

- In what ways do I fail to let God be God and instead try to exert my own control where it is not meant to be? How can I narrate one of my struggles with sin in these terms of displacing God?
- Have there been times as a parent when I was tempted to despair but rejected it, replacing it with hope? How did I do this then, and how might I continue to foster this habit?
- When have I worried for my children's futures, especially in terms of their souls and faithfulness to God and his Church? How can I bring this worry to prayer, and practice trusting God in the midst of it?

## Do

*This Week: Fasting*

Fasting is an act that should fix us more certainly and joyfully on the idea of God as God. Our small sacrifices of pleasures, comforts, and satisfaction, should remind us not only of the justice of God, but also the mercy of God. No amount of fasting could actually amend for our sins or the sins of others, but God wants so much to forgive us that he delights in our efforts, accepting them willingly as reparation in his mercy. So today, let our pangs of hunger or desire for comfort be turned upon this idea of a kind God who always desires what is best for us: himself.

# THIRD WEEK OF LENT

*Seeking and Receiving*

# THIRD SUNDAY OF LENT, YEAR A

## Read

- Exodus 17:3–7
- Psalm 95:1–2, 6–7, 8–9
  R. If today you hear his voice, harden not your hearts.
- Romans 5:1–2, 5–8
- John 4:5–42

## Reflect

As we begin this third week of Lent, we turn to the theme of seeking and receiving. There are two actions involved in this theme: a reaching out toward God, coupled with a reception of his grace. It may seem that the first is active, whereas the second is passive. But as an old African proverb states: "He who wishes to receive a coconut must catch it with his hands, not his head." In other words, even the action of receiving is something active that requires attention and intention.

Our first reading from Exodus and our Gospel passage from John both portray this theme, capturing it as a dialectic, or dialogue. Moses, flustered by and frustrated with the complaints of Israel, addresses God, then listens to the Lord's response and follows his instructions to provide them with water. And in the Gospel, the Samaritan woman, somewhat surprisingly, engages in dialogue with Jesus, asking questions and listening to his responses. Jesus may seem respectful and even kind, but he is also direct, not afraid to point out this woman's sins and willing to reveal that he is the Christ. She is not only inquisitive, but also receptive, even to the point of spreading the news to the benefit of her Samaritan community.

We are now in the thick of Lent, two and a half weeks in, but with that same amount of time still to go. At this point, Lent might start to seem impossible, especially if we feel disappointment at our inability to live our Lent as faithfully as we had hoped. On the other hand, more positively, perhaps we can look back on the past few weeks and recognize some spiritual growth and development of virtue.

To the extent that we experience the benefits of Lent, we can give the credit to God. And the great news is that this applies whether we perceive ourselves as having struggled and failed or struggled and succeeded. Failure to do Lent well can turn our focus back toward God. And success in our Lenten practices cannot be all due to ourselves, so we must thank God for that. Both our failures and successes during this time of Lent can and should bring us closer to God.

As we hear in the second reading, the Letter of Saint Paul to the Romans: "Hope does not disappoint" (Rom 5:5). We are reminded that this season is not about us, but about God. It may feel like drudgery at times, but even as we count these days of Lent, we already share in the victory of Easter, which will come regardless of how well we perceive ourselves as having lived Lent.

This is not unlike our lives as parents. At times we witness the success of our work. We see an older child reaching out to a younger one in need of help. We see the joy brought by our child's First Communion. We watch our children becoming strong and happy with the food and love we provide. But at other times, we are faced with our shortcomings as parents. We overhear a child harshly criticizing a sibling and sounding discouragingly like ourselves. We fight with a kid about attending or behaving at Mass. We seem unable to help them through an illness or injury, unsure how to get them the care they need to recover.

All of this, the good days and the bad days, work for the good if we involve God in them. We reach out to God, seeking help in times of need, thanking him for successes, and praising him through the good and the bad. And with attentiveness and intention, we prepare ourselves to receive what he gives to us, whether in the form of sufferings or consolations. We must keep the lines of communication open, conversing with Jesus as eagerly as the Samaritan woman at the well. And we must not harden our hearts when we hear his voice, even when it confronts us with our sins and failings, asking us to humble ourselves by turning ever more fully toward himself.

## Pray

Do not harden your hearts as at Meribah, as on the day of Massah in the desert. (Psalm 95:8)

## Ponder

- How is my Lent going so far? Do I recognize success or failure? How can both success and failure during Lent lead me to a closer relationship with God?
- How might I improve in seeking God? How might I improve in receiving God?
- How do I keep the lines of communication with God open in my prayer?

## Do

*This Week: Act of Contrition and Sacrament of Reconciliation*

The season of Lent is an excellent time to seek the Sacrament of Reconciliation, and it is also a great opportunity to make a habit of regular confession (often called devotional confession), as well as reciting daily the Act of Contrition, conveying our sorrow at offending God by our sins. Those of us who don't have an Act of Contrition memorized should find one today that we can keep nearby, and pray it daily. Also, we should determine when we will be able to go to confession, and put it on our calendars.

# THIRD SUNDAY OF LENT, YEAR B

## Read

- Exodus 20:1–17
- Psalms 19:8, 9, 10, 11

  R. Lord, you have the words of everlasting life.
- 1 Corinthians 1:22–25
- John 2:13–25

## Reflect

Most of us could say that we love God and want to do his will because we believe that is what is best for us. This is a beautiful beginning, but, of course, the details are more complicated. Even the Israelite people, who had been saved from slavery in Egypt, struggled with the practicalities of remaining faithful to God and doing his will. They followed Moses when they were called to leave Egypt, but they also complained on the journey and built a golden calf idol when given the opportunity. They wanted to receive the gifts of God, but they also wanted to maintain their own way of life, despite the conflict.

Today's first reading from Exodus describes God giving the law to his people in the Ten Commandments. These are not irrational or arbitrary rules. God shares this law with the people because it is what they need to flourish, to become the best versions of themselves. And yet, even when the law was so directly communicated, the people struggled to attend to it. In today's Gospel passage, we hear what had become of God's temple. This was the place where the people could worship God in the way he asked, showing that they were faithful to the commandments and honored God above all else.

Yet, Jesus saw that the people had made the temple into a marketplace. They continued to worship idols, even in this sacred space. Although the people sought to worship God on the face of it, they also wanted to maintain their own way of life, including the conflict of honoring money more than God.

We continue to struggle with this today. We love God and want to do his will, knowing that it is best for us. But sometimes when faced with choices, we prefer to take the easy way out, doing our own will even though it might not be God's. Especially as parents, we can get lost in the details of everyday life and lose sight of what matters. In part, this is because the cross of Christ, which we are called to take up, is not the easy path. However, when we seek out this cross by embracing the burdens and mundane tasks of daily life, we also receive far more than we expected.

"For the foolishness of God is wiser than human wisdom, and the weakness of God is stronger than human strength" (1 Cor 1:25). This description of Christ crucified is a beautiful reminder from our second reading as we begin this third week of Lent. Similarly, family life, with all its struggles, may not always appear wise to others, and it may expose our weaknesses. But because we seek Christ, we also receive abundantly through Christ.

## Pray

God so loved the world that he gave his only Son. (John 3:16)

## Ponder

- How do I seek to do God's will, but sometimes hold myself back by other concerns or desires?
- When have I had false idols? How do I avoid getting lost in the details of life so as to keep my focus on love of God?

- When have I felt that family life exposed my weaknesses? When have I received generously from God?

**Do**

*This Week: Act of Contrition and Sacrament of Reconciliation*

The season of Lent is an excellent time to seek the Sacrament of Reconciliation, and it is also a great opportunity to make a habit of regular confession (often called devotional confession), as well as reciting daily the Act of Contrition, conveying our sorrow at offending God by our sins. Those of us who don't have an Act of Contrition memorized should find one today that we can keep nearby, and pray it daily. Also, we should determine when we will be able to go to confession and put it on our calendars.

# THIRD SUNDAY OF LENT, YEAR C

**Read**

- Exodus 3:1–8a, 13–15
- Psalm 103:1–2, 3–4, 6–7, 8, 11
  R. The Lord is kind and merciful.
- 1 Corinthians 10:1–6, 10–12
- Luke 13:1–9

**Reflect**

A call to conversion is at the heart of Lent. Lent is a penitential season, but penance is about more than making amends for sin. It is about reforming our lives in such a way that we give gratitude to God and recognize our many blessings, including the blessing of hardship. In this way, we can become who God intends us to be, and ultimately this meaningfulness of being a child of God also helps us to become happier. Thus, when we hear passages such as those in today's readings, we need not fall into a bout of negativity or despair, but rather recall that the conversion associated with penance helps us to become our best selves.

In today's Gospel reading from Luke, we hear Jesus calling the people to repentance and warning that they will perish if they do not repent. Likewise, our second reading today warns against making the mistakes made by Moses and the Israelite people. Both passages can sound like dire warnings; at the very least, we can detect the urgency in these readings. We must not delay or procrastinate in acknowledging our sins, but face up to them boldly.

Nobody is perfect, and perhaps our lives as parents have really brought home the message that we have many flaws. Yet, we are still beloved children of God, and that is the reason for Jesus' urgency and Paul's words to the Corinthians. There is an old African proverb that the one who wishes to receive a coconut falling from a tree must prepare his hands, so he does not catch it with his head. We should not underestimate the importance of our readiness to receive.

God's grace is abundant, and God always wants what is best for us. God wants to give us every good gift. But to be able to receive those gifts, we must ready our hearts. This means acknowledging our sins and failings and truly repenting of them. Contrition involves the sorrow for our sins that we've identified, but it also leads us to acts of penance, including the willingness to bear the misfortunes and challenges of our lives as parents. Penance is a way that we seek out the God we love and who loves us. And this seeking will allow us to receive, and to recognize, the blessings that God has given us in our family life.

### Pray

Merciful and gracious is the Lord. (Psalm 103:8A)

### Ponder

- When was a time that I faced up to my mistakes? How was it painful? How did it allow me to move forward fruitfully?
- When have I delayed or procrastinated in addressing my sins or weaknesses? Is there any particular sin that I should be addressing more actively now through penance and trying to change?
- How do we live our lives in a way that demonstrates our belief that God wants to give us every good gift as his

beloved children? How do we ready ourselves to receive God's graces through penance?

**Do**

*This Week: Act of Contrition and Sacrament of Reconciliation*

The season of Lent is an excellent time to seek the Sacrament of Reconciliation, and it is also a great opportunity to make a habit of regular confession (often called devotional confession), as well as reciting daily the Act of Contrition, conveying our sorrow at offending God by our sins. Those of us who don't have an Act of Contrition memorized should find one today that we can keep nearby, and pray it daily. Also, we should determine when we will be able to go to confession and put it on our calendars.

# MONDAY

## Read

- 2 Kings 5:1–15AB
- Psalm 42:2, 3; 43:3, 4

  R. A thirst is my soul for the living God.
- Luke 4:24–30

## Reflect

Today's first reading from the Second Book of Kings tells the story of Naaman the Syrian, who was healed of his leprosy by Elisha, the Jewish prophet. In the Gospel passage from Luke, Jesus makes reference to this story of Naaman. Jesus' point concerns the rejection of prophets by their own people. In this telling, Jesus is implying his own rejection, which is vividly depicted after he concludes. This theme of Jesus' rejection by his own people recurs throughout the season of Lent.

But what might we, who name ourselves Christians and claim Jesus as our Savior, take from such stories? If we can envision ourselves as the ones who, like Mary Magdalene, embraced Christ and believed with heartfelt conversion, we must also attempt to see ourselves as the ones who have rejected Jesus in our daily sins. Very few believed the prophets and heeded their words; the vast majority were decided against what they perceived as a threat. And so also with Jesus; his rejection by so many of the people becomes clearly evident in his passion and crucifixion.

Inasmuch as we allow our familiarity in our faith to tend toward complacency, we become part of the majority in these stories. Out of his desperation, Naaman seeks out a prophet of Israel. Though he is skeptical and even critical of Elisha's treatment plan for his leprosy, he undertakes it. And Naaman's healing is beyond the physical cure to his leprosy; it also inspires in him faith in the God of Israel.

As much as we dislike being in situations of desperation, they do at least seem to awaken in us the need for seeking God. They shake us from our complacency, making us aware of our hopelessness without God. Although we may become somewhat hardened to the difficulties of raising children, there are also many times when we experience a feeling of desperation or hopelessness, from something as seemingly silly as a child who will not stay asleep during the night to a toddler who has "gone missing" somewhere in the house … or possibly out of it? From a tantrum at the grocery store to a trip to the ER, parenting can sometimes entail this feeling of dire need.

In this third week of Lent, let us be sure to use these experiences as opportunities to seek God with our whole hearts, echoing the words of the psalmist: "My soul thirsts for God, the living God" (Ps 42:3). Nor should we allow only the extreme situations to lead us to reach out to God in prayer. No matter how used to our daily struggles we become, we must try to involve Jesus in them. Recalling the brief daily prayers included in this book is a great way to remember God throughout our day, during those moments of quiet, chaos, and everything in between.

## Pray

My soul thirsts for God, the living God. (Psalm 42:3)

## Ponder

- When have I had a moment of desperation that led me to cry out to God for help?
- When have I let familiarity in daily life lead me to complacency and even a rejection of God exhibited in my sins?

- How can I work to seek God in my daily life — not only in situations of extreme need, but also in the everyday challenges and blessings?

## Do

*This Week: Act of Contrition and Sacrament of Reconciliation*

We know that we sometimes fall into complacency and decide not to bother with prayer until we hit a moment of dire need. Take a moment to consider such failures that lead us to reject Jesus and the challenges and sufferings he presents. Let us ask God for forgiveness with an Act of Contrition. Then we can try to find a specific way to amend for this in order to increase our recollection of God's presence in the daily moments of life; for example, writing prayers on notes around the house, setting the lock screen on our phones to a holy image or scriptural verse, or setting an alarm to serve as a reminder.

# TUESDAY

## Read

- Daniel 3:25, 34–43
- Psalm 25:4–5AB, 6 and 7BC, 8–9
  R. Remember your mercies, O Lord.
- Matthew 18:21–35

## Reflect

Both of our readings today convey a sort of desperation. In Daniel, we find the recognition of the people's sin, as well as the consequences of that sin. Sin is always a rejection of God at some level, and that rejection often continues when we ignore, deny, or minimize our sin. Azariah's words, however, convey the opposite. Acknowledging sin and its consequences brings Azariah to beg God for mercy, for forgiveness. He notes the Lord's past faithfulness and mentions how God's kindness and mercy in delivering them will bring glory to God.

In the Gospel of Matthew, Jesus responds to Peter's question of forgiveness with an image of the kingdom of God that involves a king graciously forgiving a large debt. This is a powerful representation of how God deals with us in our sin. When we plead for forgiveness of our sins, he responds with gracious compassion. The implications, however, extend beyond God forgiving our sins to also involve a command that we must forgive the sins of others who are in debt to us by their sins against us.

During this season of Lent, and especially during this week, we focus on acknowledging our sins and asking forgiveness in the Act of Contrition and Sacrament of Reconciliation. We recognize that our sins truly are offenses against the God we love so much, and when we understand that, we rightly feel an urgency to be forgiven. Thus, we take comfort in the knowledge that God also loves us and wants to forgive us, if only we are willing to admit our debt and ask for that mercy. And yet, we can also see how crucial it is that we be willing to forgive others.

It almost seems natural to hold grudges against those who have offended us. And, at times, these people who have offended us are our own family members, including a spouse, children, mother, father, or siblings. We might accurately note the injustice of someone's sin against us, particularly in family life, where respect and kindness should be intrinsic to our home. We thus rightly feel indignation when our children complain, insult us, or disobey us. However, we are called beyond being "right" in these matters to being merciful and forgiving. After all, God is always right in the consequences of sin we experience or the justice of punishing our offenses against him. Yet we see that God deals kindly with the sinner nonetheless. Nor does this contradict his justice; rather, his mercy goes beyond mere justice, as should ours.

From day to day, we often build expectations on the past failings of our family members, coming to expect certain "offenses," and we judge a person even in advance of his or her actions. Again, while this may be natural and even just in its own way, we are called to something more as followers of Jesus. If we want to embrace our role in the kingdom of God, we must strive to live as Jesus did. In a situation of extreme injustice, he embraced his cross, even praying for those who persecuted him and dying for the forgiveness of all our sins.

While we feel the desperation that brings us to God, begging forgiveness for our sins, let us also recognize that others — even our children or spouse — may feel desperation when they recognize their own faults, sins, and failings. We want to raise our children with the understanding that they can always begin again, that no sin is the end, and that a mistake is merely the beginning of improvement. Our loving forgiveness is instrumental in fostering this growth in them, and when we reflect on God's forgiving ourselves, we become better at making the effort to forgive our children.

**Pray**

Do not put us to shame, but deal with us in your kindness and great mercy. (Daniel 3:41–42)

**Ponder**

- Is there a situation in which I find myself slow to forgive, preferring rather to hold a grudge? Do I do this in family life, letting my negative expectations count against my children or spouse?
- Do I let desperation at my own sins bring me closer to God? Do I recognize my mistakes as the beginning of improvement, with the help of God?
- When do I hold on to being "right" rather than being kind and forgiving? What would change if I focused on mercy rather than justice?

**Do**

*This Week: Act of Contrition and Sacrament of Reconciliation*

Before praying our Act of Contrition today, we should take a moment to reflect on how sin can bring a feeling of desperation and yet, how willing God is to forgive us if we are willing to ask. Just as God will not refuse his mercy to a penitent heart, so also we must be willing to practice mercy toward those who offend us, including our children and spouse.

# WEDNESDAY

## Read

- Deuteronomy 4:1, 5–9
- Psalm 147:12–13, 15–16, 19–20
  R. Praise the Lord, Jerusalem.
- Matthew 5:17–19

## Reflect

We are often led to believe that Jesus in the New Testament dismissed all the strange restrictions of the Jewish people. We often hear people explaining that the people of Jesus' time tended toward legalism, in the worst sense of it — the desire to follow the law, simply for the law's sake, with no higher motivation and no passion for the significance of these rules. However, while Moses emphasizes the importance of the law in the first reading from Deuteronomy, Jesus also recognizes the importance of the law. And we are led to reflect on what he means when he states that he has come not to abolish, but to fulfill.

Sadly, Catholicism often appears to outsiders — and even to members of the Church — as merely a collection of laws and restrictions that primarily end in making people miserable. And if we were simply to look at a list of various rules of the Church, we can see how they might appear that way on paper. Furthermore, we may also have encountered people who feel slighted or who are personally suffering the impact of a particular Church regulation. At times, the restrictions of the Church, and their perceived negative impact, may even lead people away from the Church.

And yet, we cannot reflect on today's readings without pausing to consider why Moses and Jesus would both view the statutes of God in a positive manner. Could it be that these are more than just annoying restrictions? It certainly seems so when we look at the words of Moses. The laws guide the people, enabling them to be successful in a new land, as well as drawing the praise of others for their wisdom in following these laws. We see that God wants the people to flourish, and the laws of God are instrumental in bringing about this flourishing.

Jesus is of this tradition, with reverence for the law. Although at times he recognizes a problem with the loyalty to regulations rather than the acknowledgment of God's intention in gifting the law, nonetheless Jesus does not see himself as destroying the tradition. He is the Messiah who fulfills the law and the prophets.

What does this mean for us? On the one hand, we must face the fact that our Catholic Faith does have many rules and regulations. Perhaps in this season of Lent we feel more acutely aware of them; we are required to abstain from meat on Friday and to offer a daily Lenten sacrifice as well. Yet, hopefully we also recognize that this injunction to do penance is aimed at facilitating our freedom and flourishing as beloved children of God. Rather than limiting us by restricting our choices, penance allows us to grow and improve, aligning our will with God's in a way that ultimately makes us holier … and happier.

We take great inspiration from and comfort in the fact that Jesus shares with us in all the sufferings of daily life. His fulfilling of the law and prophets came in the form of his own sharing in human life and faith, even to following the rules and regulations of the tradition. And yet, we also know that it was so much more than that.

People often misunderstand our motivations to emphasize family life in the Catholic tradition. The Sacrament of Marriage brings with it an obligation to be open to children and to raise them in the Catholic Faith. It is a burden in some sense, as we recognize the struggles and difficulties that come with children. It's no wonder that outsiders might be skeptical of our choice to have children — or "so many" children. And we shouldn't be surprised if others are unsympathetic to these burdens of family life that we have taken upon ourselves. Nor would it be appropriate for us to respond by explaining our children as simply our following of the law.

Whether others can see it or not, our children and our family life as given us by God are more than burdens of the law; these are gifts aimed at facilitating our freedom. While children often bring us great joy, they may also restrict our choices and appear to squash our personal flourishing in some ways. This calls us beyond the selfishness we could potentially find ourselves trapped in. We may not easily dine out at expensive restaurants nor live in a pristine upscale house, but we have the opportunity for freedom in doing the will of God in a particular way, as parents who generously respond to the needs of others in a loving gift of self.

## Pray

Your law is my delight.

## Ponder

- What is a law or rule that I have a hard time following? Why do I tend to devalue or ignore this rule? Is it of any consequence naturally or supernaturally?
- Do I have a tendency toward legalism that strips the law of its meaning and call to freedom? Do I see the gift behind the rules and wisdom of God in them? Do I explain them as such to my children?
- How does the idea of rules facilitating freedom fit into my understanding of Lent as a season of penance?

**Do**

*This Week: Act of Contrition and Sacrament of Reconciliation*

It is a usual practice to have the examination of conscience reflect on the Ten Commandments of the Old Testament or perhaps the Beatitudes found in the Gospels of Matthew or Luke. While there are limitations on this, it is good to acknowledge that when we make our Act of Contrition, we are expressing contrition for the breaking of laws given to us as gifts to facilitate our freedom and flourishing as children of God.

# THURSDAY

## Read

- Jeremiah 7:23–28
- Psalm 95:1–2, 6–7, 8–9

  R. If today you hear his voice, harden not your hearts.
- Luke 11:14–23

## Reflect

"But if it is by the finger of God that I drive out demons, then the kingdom of God has come upon you," says Jesus in today's passage from the Gospel of Luke. Even after witnessing an amazing healing, driving out a mute demon from a man who then could talk, the crowds seem incredulous of Jesus, confused at who he might be. They fail to recognize that the kingdom of God has come upon them, that Jesus is the kingdom of God in person. We can almost detect a bit of frustration in his explanation to the crowds.

Nor would this be the first time that people fail to recognize or appreciate the Lord. We see that this rejection of God is a long-standing tendency. The prophet Jeremiah also describes rejection on the part of the people, who were commanded to listen to God and walk in his ways, yet chose instead to turn their backs on him, refusing to listen to his voice or take correction.

Is it stubbornness, laziness, or disbelief that leads us to reject God's call in our lives? It may be any of these. We love to have control, to have everything our own way, according to our own plans and desires. Faith is demanding. Heeding the command of God often means letting go of our selfish wants and tendency to do whatever everyone else is doing. Part of the incredulity in response to Jesus stems from the accurate perception that recognizing Jesus as the kingdom of God would change everything. Fear is thus an understandable reaction; faith in Jesus is life-changing. It is easier to reject the truth than to embrace the demands of belief. We have a tendency to harden our hearts when we hear the voice of the Lord calling us to share in the suffering of Christ.

Yet, during this season of Lent, we are asked precisely to enter into that journey. We remember Jesus' days of temptation by the Devil in the desert, his long walk under the weight of the cross, and his unjust crucifixion. As parents, however, we are uniquely suited to embrace the cross; we are often faced with involuntary burdens. Seldom do we wake up hoping for or expecting a tantrum because of handing a toddler the wrong spoon. We can't anticipate the call home from the school nurse about a sickness or injury requiring an immediate pickup. We may have no desire to do mountains of laundry. And, at times, we may even wonder what has become of us … we used to seem so normal — regular people with unique interests who were fun to know. Now, it's a genuine, unending life of service.

And how could it be any better, if we want to heed God's voice? We can make the best of this! We see in Jesus a life of service, a life directly lived for others, and now we have the opportunity also to live a life of service for others. When we decide to narrate it positively as a participation in Jesus' life, the little tasks that might otherwise appear menial or monotonous can be occasions for joy.

Belief in Christ changes everything because it brings meaning to all of those daily acts we do. Parents of all beliefs and even un-belief perform these same tasks. Yet, we are empowered by our faith in Christ; these little acts of love we do as parents are not insignificant. There is far more to be gained than there is to be lost when we unite our sufferings to Christ.

## Pray

Do not harden your hearts as at Meribah, as on the day of Massah in the desert. (Psalm 95:8)

## Ponder

- How do I reject God's call in minor ways throughout my day, perhaps when confronted with the involuntary sacrifices I must make on behalf of my family?
- How has my seeking Christ in the midst of everyday parenting allowed me to receive graces? How has keeping a deeper meaning in mind brought joy to the little tasks?
- Has there been a time when a child has seemed to subvert my intention of creating a Christian home? How did I respond to him or her, and how might I respond better?

## Do

*This Week: Act of Contrition and Sacrament of Reconciliation*

Every sin can be seen as rooted in a rejection of God, who is our beginning and our end, and to whom we owe everything. As we say our Act of Contrition today, recognize this contrition as an acceptance of God, a refusal to reject God, a refusal to harden our hearts against his call to unite our suffering with Christ's.

# FRIDAY

## Read

- Hosea 14:2–10
- Psalm 81:6C–8A, 8BC–9, 10–11AB, 14, and 17
  R. I am the Lord your God: hear my voice.
- Mark 12:28–34

## Reflect

In today's Gospel reading, Jesus responds to a scribe's question about the greatest commandment by quoting the Shema prayer, an important daily piece of Jewish piety. It is remarkable in its simplicity. We hear that the greatest command is simply to love God, and the second is to love our neighbor as ourselves.

We often complicate life and our Christian faith by getting lost in the details. It's not that details are insignificant. Indeed, they are often crucial and necessary if we want to follow God faithfully. On the other hand, it is possible to get so caught up in rules, opinions, the faults of others, conflicts in the Church, and our own sins that we lose sight of this greatest commandment. And what is Lent if not an opportunity to grow in love for God? All of our good intentions and strict Lenten discipline will come to very little if they are not part of our efforts to love God with our heart, mind, soul, and strength.

But how do we do this, especially when we find ourselves in the midst of responsibilities of family life and housework? We see the answer also in the Gospel reading. It is almost as though the scribe wants to test Jesus, to see how he will respond given that the answer should be obvious. Jesus' answer shows that he works from inside the Jewish tradition, with respect for the faith. But just as Jesus seems to pass the scribe's test, we wonder whether Jesus might not also be testing the scribe. The scribe agrees with Jesus' words! This seems to indicate an acceptance of Jesus. Indeed, the scribe gives him the title "teacher," or rabbi, when he responds, and we see that the scribe seems to pass Jesus' test, as one with understanding, not far from the kingdom of God.

When we find ourselves lost in our lives as parents, we are given this opportunity: to converse with Jesus. We see in the Gospel story understanding and even relationship; there is profound agreement between Jesus and the scribe who sought him out to ask him this question. If we desire to grow in love of God, we must want to have such a relationship; we must seek Jesus in our daily lives, conversing with him and bringing him into our worst, most embarrassing moments, as well as our unexpected, joyful successes. And if we are intentional about seeking him, we must also desire to receive him, and thus we must prepare ourselves to receive God's love by being frank and open about our needs, worries, and sins.

There is no use in pretending that we are perfect or attempting to hide our mistakes in this relationship. God sees all. God recognizes our efforts and generous sacrifices. He knows our challenges and our difficulties. He knows our various disappointments in ourselves, our children, our extended family. He wants to cheer us on the way, and to forgive us when we need it; but for it to be truly effective, we have to desire that forgiveness and the conversion of heart that comes with accepting God's unconditional love.

We can easily overcomplicate Lent, piling up resolutions and mechanically adhering to these decisions. We want to do it all, with the best of intentions. Yet, even doing it all is doing little without this foundational love of God. We might take the scribe as our example. We can seek out Jesus throughout our days, recalling his conversation with the scribe. Jesus is our teacher, too, and we can grow in love by keeping in mind that our daily acts as parents, and the sacrifices of Lent, are ways of loving.

**Pray**
Love the Lord with all your heart, all your mind, all your soul, and all your strength. (see Mark 12:30)

**Ponder**

- How has Lent given me the opportunity to grow in my relationship with Jesus? How have I succeeded in conversing with the Lord in the midst of daily life?
- How can I renew my intention to make my Lenten resolutions about loving God better? How has my love for God prevented devotional practices from becoming routine?
- Have I ever allowed the details of the faith or my concerns and worries about life to get between me and that foundational love of God?

**Do**
*This Week: Act of Contrition and Sacrament of Reconciliation*
Rote memorization and routine confession are never the point when it comes to the Act of Contrition or Sacrament of Reconciliation. This prayer and this sacrament have meaning as expressions of love for God. They are ways of loving God, seeking him out even in our failings. Moreover, they are key ways that we also receive God's grace; we cleanse ourselves so that we are open to a loving relationship with God. Let us keep this in mind today as we pray our Act of Contrition.

# SATURDAY

## Read

- Hosea 6:1–6
- Psalm 51:3–4, 18–19, 20–21AB

  R. It is mercy I desire, and not sacrifice.
- Luke 18:9–14

## Reflect

The dangers of hypocrisy seem built into practicing the faith. For as much as we desire to be faithful Catholics, we also know we will slip up. At such times, an outside observer might think we are living hypocritically even though we're aware of our failures and trying to overcome them. What delight people seem to have in identifying someone as a hypocrite!

The season of Lent, with its penitential practices, can make us acutely aware of this concern. Even on Ash Wednesday we encounter some irony, if not contradiction. On the very day we are given ashes on our forehead, we are told to pray in secret and not let others know we are fasting. And now, on this Saturday of the third week of Lent, we hear Hosea's words that God desires love, not sacrifice. The contrast in the Gospel is also striking; the Pharisee who observes the faith so strictly nevertheless appears unfavorably in comparison with the humble tax collector.

Thus we may ask ourselves, how are we supposed to live our Lent well? For if we adhere well to our resolutions and intentions, we may become prideful like the Pharisee. But failing to make an effort doesn't seem to be what God desires either. Nor do we want to seek out a life of sin, such as becoming a dishonest tax collector in order to find humility. A negative perspective shows us trapped in every way when it comes to doing penance well.

And yet, this is not the ultimate message of today's readings! If we can imagine a pessimistic reading, we should also work to develop a more optimistic understanding. We know the rejoicing that happens in heaven over a repentant sinner. And we also know that the judgment of our penance truly rests in the hands of God, not to the casual or curious observers of our lives. While others may be able to accuse us of being hypocritical or think they detect insincerity in our attempts to live a holy life, we cannot be guided by this judgment.

This is a good reminder for us as parents. Undertaking family life opens us up to many criticisms for our choices: attachment parenting or not; Catholic school, homeschool, or public school; free-range parenting; activity choices; faith formation; family size; etc. It's natural and easy to be sensitive, especially in those beginning years when we feel we have to and ought to be able to get everything right. As time goes on, we realize the sheer impossibility of perfection in parenting life. We know that sometimes our children don't eat as healthy as they should or have too much screen time or demonstrate a lack of compassion for others. Fighting against exhaustion, we may find ourselves out of patience, inconsiderate of friends or family, and not spending the time we want in prayer. And yet, despite all this, we still want to be good Catholics, witnessing positively to the faith that we believe. We love God, and that should not be underestimated!

The great news is that we truly can be good Catholics, even with all of our mistakes. We may at times get misinterpreted as hypocritical Pharisees, but even this can be an advantage! Our Lenten sacrifices, whether lived perfectly in a true spirit of love of God and genuine conversion or lived imperfectly, can still be a cause for rejoicing in heaven. God sees and values our intentions and our effort.

## Pray

My sacrifice, O God, is a contrite spirit. (Psalm 51:19)

## Ponder

- When am I concerned about being labeled a hypocrite? How have I let go of that fear so I can concentrate more fully on loving God and doing his will?
- How has being unable to achieve perfection in family life opened a possibility of true humility? How have my failures helped me to turn to God more often?
- Was there a time when I judged others unfairly, criticizing their parenting or practice of the Faith? When have I made an effort to view the actions of others charitably?

## Do

*This Week: Act of Contrition and Sacrament of Reconciliation*

Today is Saturday, a day typically associated with the Sacrament of Reconciliation, as the day when most parishes make that sacrament available. Confession is a beautiful and powerful sacrament, and, in this season of Lent, it's both appropriate and truly beneficial to seek God's forgiveness in this special way designated by the Church. Let us make the time today or in the very near future to get to confession (and consider bringing the whole family).

# FOURTH WEEK OF LENT

## *The Generosity and Abundance of God's Love*

# FOURTH SUNDAY OF LENT, YEAR A

## Read

- 1 Samuel 16:1B, 6–7, 10–13A
- Psalm 23:1–3A, 3B–4, 5, 6
  R. The Lord is my shepherd; there is nothing I shall want.
- Ephesians 5:8–14
- John 9:1–41

## Reflect

The season of Lent is a time of simplicity and austerity in the Church. If we are doing Lent well, we will likely feel the change in atmosphere with its somber, penitential spirit. And yet, in the midst of our sacrifices, Lenten disciplines, and the usual burdens of parenting, Lent is also a time to appreciate the abundance and generosity of God. It's a strange truth that we often feel better during Lent, as we embrace challenges and grow closer to God in love.

In the first reading from 1 Samuel, we might be led to reflect on the older brothers all being rejected as God's anointed. This selection of only one of Jesse's sons — and the youngest at that — can appear to be an affront. How can God be so choosy, preferring the unestablished youth who would appear to be least deserving? Is this not an example of stingy selectivity?

On the contrary, the selection of David — particularly as the youngest — shows the generosity of God. That God chooses any human being to be king of his people is, in fact a sign of his generosity. The choice of David remains surprising beyond today's story. While an outstanding king in many ways, David is also someone who sinned dramatically and repented wholeheartedly. We might see the foolishness of God in selecting such a person, but we know that the foolishness of God is actually wisdom.

And in his wisdom, we are all made sharers in the divine mission through Jesus' death and resurrection. Today's second reading from Ephesians tells us that we were once in darkness, but now are in light, called to live as children of the light. It is an apt image for Lent, which, in the northern hemisphere, coincides with the lengthening of daylight hours. Is it foolishness or wisdom that brings us into the life of Christ?

We know that, like David, we are sinners. Marriage and parenting seem to bring out faults that we never knew we had. And it can be hard for us to realize that we are children of the light, somehow called to share in his mission.

We know our weaknesses. Yet, in his generosity — and yes, in his wisdom — God has chosen us. He has chosen us as parents to these children of God. He has chosen us to live as children of the light in a world that often seems immersed in darkness. He provides us with an abundance of grace, even in the midst of our difficulties, and sometimes his grace finds us best when we are in the midst of such difficulties. God allows us to unite our sufferings with those of Christ, to take up our cross, and follow him. And when we commit to embracing that cross, we ultimately find that the yoke is easy, and the burden is light.

**Pray**

The Lord is my shepherd; there is nothing I lack. (Psalm 23:1)

**Ponder**

- Where do I see abundance and generosity in my life

during this season of Lent, including in the midst of my chosen penances and my difficulties as a parent?

- Do I see myself as chosen by God to be among the children of the light? Does this realization make my burdens seem more or less challenging?
- Which of my faults did I not fully realize until I was in the midst of family life? How do I let these failings lead me to greater dependence upon God?

**Do**

*This Week: Give Alms*

Almsgiving is one of the three traditional practices of Lent. We recognize the abundance and generosity of God and seek to show this to others by willingly sharing of our financial resources, even — especially — when it causes sacrifice on our part. Moreover, every needy person we encounter is an opportunity for us to remember the poverty of our God in becoming human and choosing to suffer and die at the hands of his own people. This week, we seek out opportunities to give. Sunday might be a good day to look through our shelves and review our calendar so we can decide when we might contribute to a parish or community food pantry this week.

# FOURTH WEEK OF LENT, YEAR B

**Read**

- 2 Chronicles 36:14–16, 19–23
- Psalm 137:1–2, 3, 4–5, 6

  R. Let my tongue be silenced, if I ever forget you.
- Ephesians 2:4–10
- John 3:14–21

**Reflect**

Today's Gospel passage contains one of the most famous lines of Scripture: "For God so loved the world that he gave his only Son, so that everyone who believes in him might not perish but might have eternal life" (Jn 3:16). This line is famous for good reason; it expresses so clearly God's love for us and the desire to give us eternal life, rather than destroy us according to our sins.

During this penitential season of Lent, we have many passages reminding us of the sins of the people, as well as their reluctance to accept Jesus as the Messiah. The first reading from Chronicles is one such account of the people's infidelities to God, and God's attempts to reach out to them in their sinfulness so they could redirect their lives toward him. Eventually God allowed his people to become Babylonian captives, planning to reach them in the midst of suffering and difficulty. God is persistent. He wants what is best for us and will do whatever it takes to get our attention, turning us back to himself so that we are able to recognize God's mercy and the grace through which we are saved in our life with Christ (see Eph 2:4).

We generally don't desire difficulty. In fact, many people forgo having children because they rightly recognize the many difficulties that such family life entails. Yet sometimes, God reaches us best in the midst of these challenges of parenting. Our children often expose sin struggles that might otherwise remain hidden. We may be forced to acknowledge our lack of patience, or perhaps the desire to be in control.

Recognizing these sins and weaknesses turns out to be a gift from God. It is in the midst of this brokenness that we understand our need for God and dependence upon God. Our God is generous, rich in mercy, to the point of giving his only Son in order that we might have eternal life. God always desires what is best for us, and that is himself! In loving God, we seek to do his will and thus allow ourselves to receive the abundance God offers to us.

This is not the superficial "abundance" of an expensive car or immaculate house or enviable careers. It is an abundance that sometimes involves piles of laundry, toddler smiles and laughter, teenage arguments, and bear hugs. God is with us through it all, allowing everything that has the potential to help us recognize his mercy and draw us closer to himself. He doesn't want us to be in the depths of despair or discouragement, and yet he can find us even there.

## Pray

For God so loved the world that he gave his only Son. (John 3:16)

## Ponder

- How has God reached out to me through difficulty? When has a particular parenting challenge caused me to seek God?
- How have I recognized God's abundance and generosity in my family life? Do I have current struggles where I

might do better at recalling his presence during times of trouble?

- How has having children exposed some of my failings, revealing brokenness? Have I experienced God's grace in response to this, perhaps in the Sacraments of Eucharist and Confession?

**Do**

*This Week: Give Alms*

Almsgiving is one of the three traditional practices of Lent. We recognize the abundance and generosity of God and seek to show this to others by willingly sharing of our financial resources, even — especially — when it causes sacrifice on our part. Moreover, every needy person we encounter is an opportunity for us to remember the poverty of our God in becoming human and choosing to suffer and die at the hands of his own people. This week, we seek out opportunities to give. Sunday might be a good day to look through our shelves and review our calendar so we can decide when we might contribute to a parish or community food pantry this week.

# FOURTH SUNDAY OF LENT, YEAR C

## Read

- Joshua 5:9A, 10–12
- Psalm 34:2–3, 4–5, 6–7
  R. Taste and see the goodness of the Lord.
- 2 Corinthians 5:17–21
- Luke 15:1–3, 11–32

## Reflect

The readings for this Sunday speak to us of the abundance and generosity of God. In the first passage from the Book of Joshua, we hear how the Israelite people finally begin to eat food in Canaan. It was a long sojourn in their escape from Egypt, with forty years in the desert eating nothing but manna. Yet, after such a difficult trial, they ultimately reach the promised land, with its bounty of food. The Gospel passage from Luke contains the famous parable often called "the prodigal son," wherein a younger son squanders his inheritance and then suffers for it in hunger and difficulty, deciding to return humbly to his father. This son is welcomed back lovingly and with the generosity of his father.

In both cases, people suffered as the result of their own sins, but this suffering also allowed them to recognize the abundance of God and return to him. The people of Israel had become idolatrous in Egypt, and even after they were delivered from Egypt they continued to relapse into worshipping the false gods of Egypt. Their difficult time in the desert was instrumental in allowing their return to God. Likewise, the wasteful son's experience of abusing his inheritance, resulting in poverty and a miserable life, helped in his willing return to his father.

Sometimes, we become stubborn or resentful about accepting the generosity of God. We have our own ideas about what will make us happy, and we seek to reach our goals without taking God's will into account. We can see this even in the prodigal son's older brother, who lives in the midst of abundance, with a kind and generous father, yet he can only see his own hard work without the reward he feels he deserves.

At times we may identify with the younger son, knowing that we have squandered God's gifts through our sin and need to return to God. Or we may identify with the older son, becoming resentful of all our hard work and sacrifices, failing to recognize the abundance in which we live. As parents, it is easy to identify with both! We can see our mistakes as parents, which sometimes come from our own selfishness. We also can be keenly aware of our many sacrifices and resentful of our lives of service.

These texts call us to focus on our generous and merciful Father. God wants us to flourish, and this happens when we acknowledge his abundance and are willing to receive his generosity. We may recognize God reaching out to us in many ways, from the joys of watching our children grow to the discouragement we feel on difficult days. Both of these have the power to open us to receiving the grace God intends for us, and during this season of Lent we are particularly aware of the need to confess our sins and do penance for them. "We implore you on behalf of Christ," writes Saint Paul, "be reconciled to God" (2 Cor 5:20). This second reading for today reminds us that in Christ, we are a new creation (see 2 Cor 5:17). Despite our sins and weaknesses, Christ has saved us, and God always welcomes our return.

## Pray

Taste and see that the LORD is good. (Psalm 34:9A)

## Ponder

- Where do I recognize myself in the parable of the prodigal son? When have I tended toward resentment of my duties? When have I squandered my gifts?
- Where do I see the abundance of God in my daily life? Specifically, what are some joys or challenges that have caused me to reach out for my merciful Father?
- How is God using this season of Lent to call me back to himself? How are my intentions and acts of penance helping me to be reconciled to God?

## Do

*This Week: Give Alms*

Almsgiving is one of the three traditional practices of Lent. We recognize the abundance and generosity of God and seek to show this to others by willingly sharing of our financial resources, even — especially — when it causes sacrifice on our part. Moreover, every needy person we encounter is an opportunity for us to remember the poverty of our God in becoming human and choosing to suffer and die at the hands of his own people. This week, we seek out opportunities to give. Sunday might be a good day to look through our shelves and review our calendar so we can decide when we might contribute to a parish or community food pantry this week.

# MONDAY

## Read

- Isaiah 65:17–21
- Psalm 30:2 and 4, 5–6, 11–12A, and 13B
  R. I will praise you, Lord, for you have rescued me.
- John 4:43–54

## Reflect

When we read today's readings, the message almost sounds too good to be true. God comes to the rescue. In the beautiful first reading from the Prophet Isaiah, we hear a description of the new heavens and new earth. And in the Gospel reading from John, the royal official's son is healed miraculously, and at a distance! The psalm reinforces this idea of rescue, coupled with praise and thanksgiving for our God who comes to our aid.

The healing and rescue message may not be the one we typically associate with the austere season of Lent. Isn't Lent about mortification and penance, sacrifice and willing suffering? So why, in this fourth week, do we hear readings speaking of the generosity and abundance of God?

These questions are worth further reflection as we proceed in the second half of Lent. We have here a reminder of a bigger picture, one that is so important for us to keep in mind during this penitential season. Penitential practices such as prayer, fasting, and almsgiving are never goals in themselves. We don't make our Lenten resolutions simply to make ourselves miserable, piling up sufferings for ourselves. No! Lent is about preparation for the joyous celebration of Easter, and we must try to recall that in the midst of our austerity. There is something beyond the passion and death of Jesus on the cross: his resurrection!

This is a crucial reminder for us as parents, as well. Right now we are very much "in the trenches" of family life, waging daily battles against messes, tantrums, homework, complex extracurricular schedules, and dishes. We often live without adequate sleep or time for ourselves. We make daily sacrifices that we probably never anticipated when we dreamed about having children. Our efforts don't always bring about our intended results, and sometimes we have no indication that all the work and sacrifices are amounting to anything worthwhile. We might even say that we are currently in the Lenten season of life.

In the midst of this chaos, however, we still often find joys in the blessings of our children and family life. And while we may not always feel hopeful or see any end in sight, there is purpose to our current work and sacrifices as parents. We don't always receive the immediate response to our wants, as the royal official gets his wish for his son's healing. Even when our children are grown up, we continue to worry about them or suffer from knowing their choices or misfortunes.

On the other hand, if these experiences help us to grow in humility and love for God, we will be closer to the peace described in the first reading. We will find our rescue from God — maybe not in the ways we asked or wanted, but rescue nonetheless. When we look back on these days, we will remember the moments of joy we had and recognize how God's grace was working in our lives during what may have felt like a never-ending Lent. We've probably all encountered grandparents who reminisce about the days of young children, advising parents of littles to enjoy every minute. We've heard older parents (or maybe you are the older parent) reminiscing fondly about the high school soccer games and band performances that they now miss so much. Though it's not easy to do, we should look to the abundance and generosity of God during whatever season of parenting in which we find ourselves.

**Pray**

I praise you, Lord, for you raised me up. (Psalm 30:2A)

**Ponder**

- How do I remind myself of the abundance and generosity of God in the midst of this season of penitential preparation? Have I begun thinking about my Easter celebrations, planning to help my family celebrate the feast with great joy?
- How might I benefit from keeping a broader perspective on my current struggles in family life? Do I remind myself that this stage of life does not last forever?
- What are some joys and blessings of children that I will miss in years to come? How do I remind myself to enjoy these moments now and live consciously in the present, even if I can't always identify the abundance and generosity of God in the suffering?

**Do**

*This Week: Give Alms*

Almsgiving has always been an important practice in the Church, perhaps because it so clearly is an imitation of the generosity of God for us to give to those who are in need. We can genuinely help someone, to provide some small rescue or healing. If we know we will encounter beggars this week, we can make sure to have some small bills or food items ready. If not, we might set aside this money to donate or give to a person in need later this week.

# TUESDAY

**Read**

- Ezekiel 47:1–9, 12
- Psalm 46:2–3, 5–6, 8–9

  R. The Lord of hosts is with us; our stronghold is the God of Jacob.
- John 5:1–16

**Reflect**

Today's first reading from Ezekiel provides an image of the temple of the Jewish people. The description of water indicates life, and we hear that the water flowing from the temple indeed brings growth and life to animals, fish, and fruits. Our Gospel reading from John today similarly speaks of growth and life, as Jesus heals a man who has been ill for thirty-eight years. Once again, we have readings speaking to the abundance of God and his generosity.

We hear in the Gospel reading that Jesus recognizes that the man had been ill for a long time. The question as to whether he wants to be well might seem strange. After all, that's why the man is lying by the pool that brings healing. And who wouldn't want a cure after such a long illness? The man's answer seems to provide some explanation as to why he isn't healed already, and perhaps it also hints at what he wants from Jesus. The man has no one to help him to get into the pool. Jesus, however, does not require the pool to bring healing to this man. Jesus is the living water, and in his final advice to the man, Jesus tells him he is well and not to sin anymore so that nothing worse may happen to him.

Jesus probably knew that this healing would bring about the criticism of the Jews. The Sabbath is an important day, crucial to the worship of God, and they understood it to be a day of rest from labor. Of all the practices of their tradition, Sabbath rest and worship of God was perhaps the most significant, for God himself rested on the seventh day of creation. Though the Jews were always looking for the coming of the Messiah, they would not expect a Messiah who would fail to observe this significant day of rest. Healing this man on the Sabbath seems a blatant rejection of the established tradition.

And yet, it really speaks to the generosity of God. Encountering this man who has suffered for so long, Jesus immediately wants to heal him. This is not about justice, but mercy, and such a healing is fitting for the Sabbath. After all, this day of rest is meant to bring us healing after a week of work. It reconnects us with our Creator, just as this man's healing connected him with our Redeemer. We, too, long for healing, and we find it on the new Sabbath, Easter Sunday, which celebrates Jesus' resurrection.

Once again, we are called to look beyond our sufferings of the day. Thirty-eight years was a long time for this man to suffer from a debilitating illness. As parents, we too may find ourselves immersed in a long-term trial, with no end in sight. We may feel the desperation of wanting healing or a solution to our problems, while knowing that we lack the means to solve the problem or be healed. But though the man may have been desperate, he must have still held out some hope as he lay by the pool day after day, with nothing else to do and no one to help.

As we near the end of Lent, we too must hang onto hope, looking beyond the difficulties of the day. Jesus does not solve all our problems quickly; but if we are patient, like this man, we will find abundant healing, perhaps in an unexpected way. Jesus reaches for us at our lowest moments. His grace can meet us however far down we are, and, perhaps when we least expect it, we will experience that healing and help we desire.

## Pray

God is my refuge and my strength. (see Psalm 46:2)

## Ponder

- What is one area in which I have found great difficulty, yet try to hang on to hope?
- How have I experienced the generosity of God? When have I found healing at a time when I did not expect it?
- What efforts have I made to maintain peace in the midst of difficult or stressful family life situations? How do I avoid allowing such troubles to tempt me toward sin?

## Do

*This Week: Give Alms*

It can be hard to encounter those most in need. Our society tends to push such people out of sight, such that we may rarely encounter them face to face. Despite any awkwardness of the encounter, however, such a direct experience of need is good for us, as is our willingness to give. If we know we might meet someone in need, we should be prepared to give. And if we probably won't, today is a good day to set aside some money for our Catholic Relief Services donation (the CRS Rice Bowl) and consider the poor in other parts of the world.

# WEDNESDAY

## Read

- Isaiah 49:8–15
- Psalm 145:8–9, 13CD–14, 17–18
  R. The Lord is gracious and merciful.
- John 5:17–30

## Reflect

The idea of justice is often a bit startling to us. After all, we live in a world fraught with injustice, and we hear about injustices almost daily. Most of us have also experienced some kind of injustice, though perhaps minor. And we often see people getting away with acts that they really shouldn't. So we should be excited and relieved to hear Jesus' words in the Gospel stating that the time of judgment is near, and his judgment is just. And yet, such a bold proclamation of justice often strikes a little bit of fear in us.

When we are carefully reflective, we know that if we are to be judged with complete justice, we will be found wanting. Even though we might make good efforts, the fact is that we often fall short in doing our duties with generosity and love. Little instances of selfishness creep into daily life, often in subtle ways, but sometimes even in larger ways. Especially once we have children, we find ourselves struggling with sin in new ways. We may have never thought of ourselves as angry or impatient; yet, there we are, sleep-deprived and overwhelmed, yelling so loudly the neighbors can surely hear.

It's a sobering thought in such a context that we will be judged justly by Jesus, God-made-flesh who dwelt among us. And yet, we also hear in today's reading that Jesus does not seek his own will, but the will of the one who sent him — the Father. When we consider, then, our first reading and psalm response, we have a picture of God as someone who is gracious and merciful, eager to heal and assist, extending comfort to the afflicted. So perhaps the justice of Jesus is not quite as frightening as it first appears; God's mercy reaches beyond even his justice.

In this fourth week of Lent, we are hastening toward holy week and the paschal mystery. The penances we have undertaken in acknowledgment of our sins — no matter how vigorous these penances may be — are simply not adequate "payment." We will never meet the demands of justice, especially as we continue to struggle daily with certain sins, finding only gradual improvement. Yet, the generosity and abundance of God comes to us in the midst of this recognition of our own inadequacy. God will receive our efforts as payment; in his mercy he accepts inadequate payment and forgives our debt.

Why does God deal so generously with us? It is motivated by love: "For God so loved the world that he gave his only Son, so that everyone who believes in him might not perish but might have eternal life" (John 3:16). Jesus himself is the answer to the injustice, the payment to the debt, the ultimate mercy presented to us. As Lent continues, let us keep this in mind. We cannot and will not be able to save ourselves, yet we can share in the victory if we share in the loving sacrifice made by Jesus for our salvation.

## Pray

The LORD is gracious and merciful. (Psalm 145:8A)

## Ponder

- Where do I see injustice in the world? When have I been distressed by witnessing injustice and responded to it?
- Would I be found wanting under the examination of

such justice? Do I recognize God's mercy in my life and likewise seek to extend mercy in my family life, to my spouse and children?

- When have I experienced God's love and mercy in my life? Do I live in a way that shows my conviction in God's tenderness, for example, by seeking his forgiveness in the Sacrament of Reconciliation regularly?

**Do**

*This Week: Give Alms*

Almsgiving is fundamentally about living mercy. We often see objections to charitable giving coming out of the realm of "justice." But our own experience of receiving mercy in God's forgiveness shows that our faith is not primarily about "deserving," but rather giving. And in giving to those in need, we participate in God's own work. Today, we should identify someone in need and respond with generosity, even when it requires sacrifice, as part of our Lenten journey.

---

# THURSDAY

**Read**

- Exodus 32:7–14
- Psalm 106:19–20, 21–22, 23
  R. Remember us, O Lord, as you favor your people.
- John 5:31–47

**Reflect**

Do you detect a bit of annoyance from God in the first reading from Exodus, or in Jesus' words in the Gospel reading? We might not expect to hear frustration, and yet, we should also acknowledge how justified it is, on both accounts. In the reading from Exodus, the Lord threatens to destroy the people of Israel after they have turned to idolatry in making the golden calf to worship rather than God. Jesus' frustrations come from his people's failure to recognize him as the Messiah, despite the witness of John and the Scriptures.

Perhaps we have also felt some frustration akin to this in our lives as parents. It's hard to watch our kids fail, and sometimes even harder to watch them endure the consequences. Because of that, we might — at times — try to save them from both! Moreover, there are times when they seem to be rejecting us or pushing us away, replacing the values we've tried to foster with their own idols, often built on nothing more than the whim of desire. And then there are the times that they just can't seem to get along with each other or us. Constant fighting can really drain us as parents, making our spirits feel defeated.

But the Lord should be above these feelings, right? So what are the readings today really trying to convey? Maybe our overhearing of this scolding is for our benefit. Sometimes we have a hard time taking a God's-eye perspective on a situation; we are too enmeshed in our own concerns, selfishly expecting that we can, like our children, pursue our whims and expect security and comfort with little cost. In such cases, it's good for us to know a more just perspective on our inclinations and actions.

We reject God in many ways, and God knows this. We construct our own idols, or look to those of our friends. We know Jesus is in our midst in so many different ways, from the Eucharist to those in need. And yet, we allow ourselves to be distracted from the loving relationship he offers.

If we read this scolding and take it to heart, however, we find that what lies behind it is the passionate love of God for his people. The words may seem harsh, but they are inspired by abundance and generosity. God wants so much what is best for us. God wants us to receive the gifts he offers. Jesus wants to be recognized and to be part of our lives at every moment. But God doesn't want to force us into receiving him. If we are attentive in this season of Lent, we may notice God's efforts to bring us closer to him. Let us be ready to receive those gifts and to welcome his loving sacrifice on the cross.

## Pray

Remember me, LORD, as you favor your people. (Psalm 106:4A)

## Ponder

- When have I had to experience my children's failure? How did I respond to that? Have I ever tried to save them from failing and gotten poor results?
- What are some of the idols I have in my current life? How would trying to see from a God's-eye perspective help me to recognize why they are problematic? What gifts

does the Lord want to give me?

- How have I rejected God's love? When have I received his love? How might I change my patterns of behavior so that I am more readily able to receive God's love?

**Do**

*This Week: Give Alms*

It is easy in our Lenten resolutions to become self-focused, as though the sacrifices we've undertaken, whether abstaining from food or spending extra time in prayer, are ultimately about us. Almsgiving is always other-centered, giving us the opportunity to recognize a connection with those in need. We, too, are in need, though our poverty may not be of the sort that is easily recognizable. Today, make an effort to think of those in need and how we and our families might assist them.

# FRIDAY

## Read

- Wisdom 2:1A, 12–22
- Psalm 34:17–18, 19–20, 21 and 23
  R. The Lord is close to the brokenhearted.
- John 7:1–2, 10, 25–30

## Reflect

Christ is the center of our Lent, and during such a long season of preparation, it is good to be reminded of that. Today's readings clearly draw us back to Christ — the person of Jesus, God made man, who was foretold in the Scriptures, lived among people, suffered, died, was buried, and rose again. On this Friday of Lent we have a special day of penance within a season of penance. What we say about Christmas is also true about Lent: Jesus is the reason for the season.

The first reading from the book of Wisdom seems to be a clear foreshadowing of Jesus as the Messiah. This passage dramatically portrays the thinking of the wicked in regard to the holy one, the Son of God. When we love Jesus, it can be painful for us to read these words. And yet, we might also realize that we are not unlike the crowd described in the Gospel passage. Just as they seem to judge and even dismiss Jesus as the Messiah, we have, at times, had similar jealous inclinations toward those who seem superior to us.

We often lack the humility that allows us truly to wish the best for people, and when we lose sight of Jesus or become complacent in the Faith, competitiveness can creep into our spiritual and our parenting lives. Spiritually, we may occasionally resent those people who seem to have it all together, maintaining their peace and commitment to the Faith despite difficulties. We may even feel judged by them for our own failures, in a way that makes us defensive of our sins.

When it comes to parenting, the judgment of outsiders is simply part of the job description. People judge the appearance of our kids, the success of our kids, their behavior during Mass, etc. We may be so used to this judgment that we even perceive judgment on us when there really isn't any intended!

How do we respond in a world where we naturally find competition, jealousy, and judgment? Especially during this season of Lent, we look to Christ as our example, and we work to see Christ in those around us. The implications are apparent. First, like Jesus, we can't live our lives in fear of the judgment of others. What matters most is God's perspective, and our actions must be motivated by doing his will out of our love for God. Secondly, we recognize the pain and agony endured by Jesus when he was unjustly judged and targeted by the wicked. This means we both unite our own similar sufferings to Jesus', and also that we endeavor to avoid judging others. Rather than criticizing, we seek to help. While this may at times involve advice or admonishment, almost always it involves first consideration, compassion, and assistance in sharing a burden. In such a way, we help other parents around us and strengthen the Church, the body of Christ.

## Pray

The Lord is close to the brokenhearted. (Psalm 34:19A)

## Ponder

- When have I felt judged by others for my parenting? How did I try to keep in mind that what matters is God's will and doing the best possible for my children?

- When have I found myself critical of others? How do I seek to combat that, focusing instead on ways to be helpful?
- Have I experienced feeling brokenhearted? Did I feel close to God during this suffering, knowing that Jesus also endured criticism? Did I take comfort in knowing Jesus' compassion lived out in his passion and death?

**Do**

*This Week: Give Alms*

Perhaps nothing recognizes God's intimacy with the brokenhearted as much as our own willingness to reach out to those in need. Society often wants to make such assistance conditional, implying judgment and criticism of those who require help. Today, as we look for ways to give alms, remember that God is close to the brokenhearted, including those trapped in sin.

# SATURDAY

## Read

- Jeremiah 11:18–20
- Psalm 7:2–3, 9BC-10, 11–12

  R. O Lord, my God, in you I take refuge.
- John 7:40–53

## Reflect

Nicodemus is an interesting figure. As a Pharisee and member of the Sanhedrin, he questions his fellow members who are skeptical of Jesus and critical of the crowds that seem to be recognizing Jesus as a prophet, or even the Messiah. Regardless of whatever the crowds might think Jesus to be — or even what Jesus actually is — Nicodemus sees the injustice of condemning Jesus without listening to him or finding out more information.

Though our last few days' readings have highlighted the injustice suffered by Christ, Nicodemus presents to us a voice of reason, while the crowds show us that not all of his people rejected Jesus outright. Jumping to conclusions is a tendency of our human nature! Especially when we feel threatened, as perhaps the chief priests and Pharisees felt, we are likely to make an unfair judgment on others.

Nicodemus's question suggests the possibility that they might be wrong, that there might be a genuine reason to investigate further before coming to judgment. The prejudices of those in the crowd or among the chief priests and Pharisees prevent them from seeing the big picture. It is easier to dismiss Jesus as a Galilean and dismiss Galilee as a place from which no prophet would arise.

As we close out this fourth week of Lent, we should look for ways to be more like Nicodemus. Over-discerning a situation can be problematic, but so too is the tendency to jump to conclusions, especially in forming judgments against others who seem inferior to us or different from us. This reservation of judgment extends to our own family members. It can become easy for parents to stereotype the behavior of their children, and even to make comments that betray these prejudices. Even with our own children or spouse, we don't always know the whole story, and investigation may be required.

When it comes to Christ, however, we have the faith that gives us more confidence. We see the confusion of the crowds, Nicodemus, the chief priests, and the Pharisees. But we also know the answer to their questions. Jesus is a prophet and the Messiah, God who has come among us to save us from our sins in his passion and death. It may seem surprising that God extends this intense love to us, enduring injustice out of love for us. But this is the abundance and generosity of God. Despite the injustices inherent in our daily sins against him, God continues to love us and be faithful to us, to the point of Jesus' death on the cross. The Resurrection that awaits is the ultimate sign of hope. The story doesn't end in injustice, death, and destruction; but rather, in restoration of life for all who believe.

## Pray

LORD my God, in you I trusted; save me; rescue me from all who pursue me. (Psalm 7:2A)

## Ponder

- When have I jumped to conclusions about someone, only to find out just how problematic my assumptions were? How can I be more generous in my appraisal of others?
- Do I ever stereotype my children or form judgments

about them in ways that ultimately restrict them from flourishing? When have I been charitable in interpreting the actions of my children?
- How do I take refuge in God in times of need? How do I strive to take refuge in God in times of great joy and celebration?

## Do

*This Week: Give Alms*

At times we feel certain of our opinions and lack the ability to inquire in such a way that allows greater justice. We are often kept from almsgiving by our own excuses, whether they have to do with the best options for helping the poor or our own lack of resources of time and money. Today, let us take the time to pray that God forms our hearts to resemble his own abundance and generosity, and live that out in our own generous almsgiving.

# FIFTH WEEK OF LENT

## *Embracing Difficulty and Suffering*

# FIFTH SUNDAY OF LENT, YEAR A

## Read

- Ezekiel 37:12–14
- Psalm 130:1–2, 3–4, 5–6, 7–8
  R. With the Lord there is mercy and fullness of redemption.
- Romans 8:8–11
- John 11:1–45

## Reflect

We begin this fifth week of Lent with what is often called "Lazarus Sunday," because it features the beautiful story of Jesus raising Lazarus from the dead. This also prefigures Jesus' own resurrection from the dead, illustrating God's power over death, and once again giving us reason to hope as we head into the last full week of Lent before Palm Sunday begins Holy Week.

Because we Christians believe so firmly in the resurrection of the dead and the possibility of eternal life in heaven with God, one might think that we would not be bothered by physical death. And yet, we see in this story of Lazarus that even those who firmly believe in the Resurrection are saddened by the death of Lazarus, including his sister Martha, and even Jesus, who wept in the midst of all the grieving for Lazarus. Even when we have confidence in the Resurrection, it is hard to lose someone whom we love, to continue life without them on earth. For Martha and Mary it was particularly difficult to lose their brother Lazarus because they knew that Jesus could have healed him before death came.

We sometimes think that embracing difficulty and suffering means remaining cheerful and idealistic about our trials. And yet, we see in this story something different. Losing someone we love is painful, and mourning that loss is not only a natural human reaction, but can be a holy way of embracing the difficulty: "Blessed are they who mourn, for they will be comforted" (Mt 5:4).

There is real value to having an overall optimistic and positive attitude about life, especially given our faith in Jesus' victory on the cross through his resurrection. We are also allowed to mourn and to grieve, so long as that does not become a permanent pity-party, but rather encourages us, like those in this story such as Martha and Mary, to seek Jesus in the midst of our trials. Difficulty and suffering are unavoidable in life. For those of us who are parents, we will find difficulty and suffering that we never anticipated because our hearts have been expanded with love and concern for our children. It's okay if sometimes the challenges and tragedies of family life make us sad and cause us to weep. But let us also reach out for Jesus, who has the power to heal. That healing may not come exactly as we desire, but in time we will find comfort and compassion and consolation in him.

## Pray

But you are not in the flesh; on the contrary, you are in the spirit, if only the Spirit of God dwells in you. (Romans 8:9)

## Ponder

- Have I ever experienced grief and mourning for a loved one? How did I find myself reaching out for Jesus in the midst of this?
- How does my belief in the Resurrection give me hope, but not always the emotion of happiness? How do I live

my earthly life well, including its difficulties, without losing sight of the Resurrection?

- How have I embraced difficulty and suffering in my parenting? Is there one particular situation that has caused a lot of tumult for me? How did I allow that challenge to help me grow closer to God?

## Do

*This Week: Offering Suffering*

This week we are focusing on embracing difficulty and suffering. Let us choose one particular challenge, whether a long-term burden or one of a more temporary, limited nature. This week we will be intentional about offering this suffering to God, replacing complaints with prayers of thanksgiving.

# FIFTH SUNDAY OF LENT, YEAR B

## Read

- Jeremiah 31:31–34
- Psalm 51:3–4, 12–13, 14–15
  Create a clean heart in me, O God. (Ps 51:12A)
- Hebrews 5:7–9
- John 12:20–33

## Reflect

"Unless a grain of wheat falls to the ground and dies, it remains just a grain of wheat; but if it dies, it produces much fruit" (Jn 12:24). This famous line from John's Gospel is in our readings for this fifth Sunday of Lent. When Jesus says it, he refers to his own impending suffering and death, which will draw everyone to himself and will bear fruit in the Resurrection. Yet, these words also apply to all of us; they are part of the new covenant indicated by the Prophet Jeremiah in the first reading.

The idea of "dying to one's self," which is rooted in this Gospel passage, reminds us that our challenges and difficulties can improve us in amazing ways. Jesus' resurrection could not have happened without his embrace of the difficulty and suffering of the cross. And it is through the cross that we become sharers in this new covenant. We, too, will have a physical death and the possibility of our own bodily resurrection, sharing in eternal life with God. Even now, with Jesus' model of embracing the cross, we can see in our own lives how often this pattern of cross and resurrection is repeated. Our worst sufferings are often followed by unexpected beauty and joy. Our difficulties can bear fruit that we never anticipated.

When we see the power of this perspective, we can embrace the idea of dying to ourselves. Practically speaking, this means recognizing and naming our selfishness, confessing our sins, and serving others with generosity. Family life is an ideal setting for this in many ways. We are often called upon to put our own preferences and desires to the side. We may prefer a family hike, but instead enthusiastically support the family movie time our spouse prefers. We might want to order Chinese takeout for dinner, yet willingly order the pizza that everyone else requests. We may delay our own lunch to serve a child or interrupt our work time to fix the Wi-fi for a teen who needs it for a school assignment.

During this season of Lent, we've had opportunities to reflect on our own sinfulness and to embrace penance to make amends for that. Dying to ourselves in little acts such as those named above are their own form of penance. They are not the penance of choosing a Lenten resolution, but they are the penances of seeking to do God's will through prioritizing other's needs, desires, and preferences. When we do this with generosity, we imitate Jesus' embrace of the cross.

Of course, "dying to one's self" can also be used problematically. It is not meant to impose suffering on others, nor does it excuse a lack of charity to those who are in need of assistance. Nor does God want our life on earth to be miserable and joyless. It's quite the opposite, in fact. We will encounter difficulty and suffering regardless; our lives as parents have probably driven this point home! And while there are times where we need to evaluate and solve a bad situation, there are also many times when we are called to embrace the difficulty and suffering, uniting it to Christ's cross and dying to ourselves with the hope and promise of resurrection. Oftentimes, our generosity in such situations ultimately contributes to our joy, rather than detracting from it.

## Pray

Have mercy on me, God, in accord with your merciful love. (Psalm 51:3)

## Ponder

- When have I had difficulty in identifying whether to solve a problem or to embrace it as a cross? Have I ever set up false crosses for myself, by delaying addressing an issue within family life?
- Where do I succeed in dying to myself? Do I yield my own preferences in order to show love to my children and spouse?
- When have I responded cheerfully and generously to sacrifices, uniting them to Christ's cross instead of complaining about them? How do I try to cultivate my perspective of generosity in dying to myself?

## Do

*This Week: Offering Suffering*

This week we are focusing on embracing difficulty and suffering. It might be helpful to choose one particular challenge. It might be a long-term burden, or it could be one of a more temporary, limited nature. Be intentional about offering this suffering to God, replacing complaining about it with prayers of thanksgiving.

# FIFTH SUNDAY OF LENT, YEAR C

## Read

- Isaiah 43:16–21
- Psalm 126:1–2, 2–3, 4–5, 6
  R. The Lord has done great things for us; we are filled with joy.
- Philippians 3:8–14
- John 8:1–11

## Reflect

We are nearing the end of Lent, and today we read Paul's words in our second reading: "Just one thing: forgetting what lies behind but straining forward to what lies ahead, I continue my pursuit toward the goal, the prize of God's upward calling, in Christ Jesus" (Phil 3:13–14). This is a great reminder for us as we seek to live these last few weeks of Lent. We are continuing forward, with a goal. Ultimately, we recognize the prize as sharing in the joy of Christ's resurrection on Easter Sunday. But we know that the difficulty and suffering of Jesus' passion and death come before that.

"Straining forward to what lies ahead" is a key idea of our faith. We see this also in today's Gospel passage about the woman caught in adultery. Jesus, however, doesn't succumb to the Pharisees' game in trying to test him. When they've given up and left, he tells the woman that he doesn't condemn her. But he also says, "Go, and from now on do not sin any more" (Jn 8:11). In other words, Jesus calls this woman to move forward, rather than dwelling in darkness.

As parents, we too must strive to move forward. Like anyone else, we make mistakes. Sometimes we can see these play out in our children, such as when they pick up our bad habits or react to our stress and frustration. Lent reminds us of our sin and our lives as sinners. But it also reminds us of our upward calling, in Christ Jesus. Penance is a gift; it is an amazing opportunity to address our sins of the past and move beyond them.

Lent is a season of voluntary penance; we choose a resolution, a sacrifice that shows our desire and willingness to make amends for our sin and refocus our attention on Jesus. Parenting, however, provides us with many opportunities for involuntary penances — not just during Lent, but year-round! When we forgo our own desires and preferences and embrace the difficulties and challenges of our lives, we also make amends for our sins and respond to our upward calling.

Embracing our difficulties and sufferings is one way that we share in the sufferings of Christ and become conformed to his death, as Saint Paul writes, and in this way we will also attain resurrection from the dead (see Phil 3:10). Like many of our other intentions and goals, we won't always succeed in this; like Paul, we don't have "perfect maturity" (Phil 3:12) We may sometimes grumble and complain, push our troubles onto others, or procrastinate in addressing both our challenges and our failings as parents. Yet, in hope, we see how even this can help us to grow closer to God; the knowledge of our sins opens us to that opportunity for involuntary penance, lived out in the context of family life. When we strain forward, we unite our struggles to Christ's cross, in response to that upward calling, and the joyful knowledge that the Resurrection follows the crucifixion!

## Pray

The LORD has done great things for us; Oh, how happy we were! (Psalm 126:3)

## Ponder

- How do I remind myself to move forward, to get up again after a struggle, and to remember the prize of God's calling?
- What are some opportunities for involuntary penances that I have faced in the past as a parent? What are some current challenges that I could embrace as penances?
- When have I done well at remembering Jesus and uniting my struggles to his cross? For the future, how can I help myself to look beyond present difficulties and instead strain forward? How does the knowledge of resurrection help me to stay positive?

## Do

*This Week: Offering Suffering*

This week we are focusing on embracing difficulty and suffering. It might be helpful to choose one particular challenge. It might be a long-term burden, or it could be one of a more temporary, limited nature. Be intentional about offering this suffering to God, replacing complaining about it with prayers of thanksgiving.

# MONDAY

## Read

- Daniel 13:1–9, 15–17, 19–30, 33–62
- Responsorial Psalm 23:1–3A, 3B–4, 5, 6
  R. Even though I walk in the dark valley I fear no evil; for you are at my side.
- John 8:1–11

## Reflect

Over and over again in stories from the Old and New Testaments, we find that good people are not spared from difficulty. Today's first reading from Daniel is an especially stark example of this. Susanna is a good and holy woman, a daughter of Israel who lives righteously. And yet, this does not prevent her from being falsely accused by elders who want to take advantage of her sexually and then punish her for her refusal. Although in the end God does hear her prayer, and she is vindicated by the wisdom of Daniel in examining the two elders separately, Susanna is not spared the ordeal of being falsely accused and facing the very real possibility that her life will end as the result of this false accusation.

Psalm 23, our responsorial psalm for the day, indicates something very similar. In this well-known psalm, we find the image of the Lord as a shepherd, with us in the dark valley, giving courage in times of troubles, protecting us from adversaries. Thus, once again, we find that those who trust in God are not exempt from problems, concerns, or challenges. The prayer of Psalm 23 is written in such a way that it almost seems to be a reminder for people who are facing great difficulties. It is an anthem for times of confusion, doubt, or anxiety, bringing consolation in the knowledge that God is with us as we face trouble.

As we draw ever closer to the end of Lent, we can anticipate what lies ahead with Holy Week, when we enter into the passion and death of Jesus. Not even Jesus, God with us, was spared from difficulty in this life on earth. Nor will we ever find ourselves in an easy life, completely free of suffering. Given this, we must ask ourselves how we want to respond to difficulty and suffering.

Susanna might have easily responded with resentment when she was caught in such a predicament. Rather than avoiding sin and turning to God in faith, she might have complained of the injustice and turned away from God in anger. And Jesus, in the constant rejection he faced from his own people, might have tried to force or manipulate them to believe. Instead, however, he allowed the rejection and ultimately embraced the suffering of the cross.

As parents, we will face a lot of difficulty and suffering that seem undeserved and unfair. From financial sacrifices for our children to watching our children suffer from illness or the treatment of bullies, we will encounter many challenges. Our response to these should be like that of Susanna, voiced in the confidence of Psalm 23. We won't let the challenges drive us away from God, but rather we will embrace the difficulty and suffering, seeing them as God's way of trying to draw us ever closer to himself.

## Pray

Even though I walk through the valley of the shadow of death, I will fear no evil, for you are with me. (Psalm 23:4AB)

## Ponder

- Have I ever responded with resentment to a difficulty or challenge rather than embracing it willingly? Did I find a difference in my peace when I finally ended my denial and accepted the situation?

- Have I ever found God's support and help in surprising ways when I put my trust in him in the midst of difficulty? How did that encourage me for the future, giving me a cause for hope?
- How have I found difficulties and sufferings to lead me to Christ? Where do I still need to work on allowing these challenges to help me depend on God?

## Do

*This Week: Offering Suffering*

What challenges are facing us today or this week? Let us take some time to return to that particular struggle identified yesterday or to identify a specific concern we know we have encountered or will encounter today. How can we be intentional about offering that difficulty to God? How can we anticipate the challenge and prepare our hearts to react to the suffering in a holy way?

---

# TUESDAY

**Read**

- Numbers 21:4–9
- Psalm 102:2–3, 16–18, 19–21

  R. O Lord, hear my prayer, and let my cry come to you.
- John 8:21–30

**Reflect**

"The people's patience was worn out by the journey" (Nm 21:4) might be one of the best descriptions for what we often feel as parents. Nor should it come as a surprise that the Israelites became weary with their trek through the desert; we dare not romanticize their escape from Egypt as something easy and wonderful. It was tough, and their response was resentment and complaining.

There is a natural human tendency to lose our patience and complain during times of difficulty. Yet, while this is a natural response of our fallen human nature, God wants and expects a supernatural response in times of trouble. He knows that what is best for our happiness and holiness is a larger perspective for us to regard suffering as drawing us closer to him. The Israelite people had obvious reasons to maintain such a supernatural perspective. After all, they had witnessed the plagues against Egypt and were saved through the miraculous parting of the Red Sea. Rather than continuing to dwell and reflect on God's saving them so dramatically, they turned from gratitude to the realities of their bodily discomfort. Even after God had given them so much, they lacked the willingness to give back to God in their difficulties.

When we reflect on our own lives, we also can probably detect the movements of God's grace. We may not have the dramatic and miraculous in our personal histories, but we often can see how God led us to our spouse, protected us in some great difficulty, or guided us to make certain choices that turned out to have a positive effect on our lives. And yet, we lose sight of these blessings when we find ourselves immersed in the challenges of parenting. In the midst of all our daily sacrifices, our patience worn out by the journey, we easily resort to complaining.

It may not seem encouraging, then, that God punishes the Israelites for their complaints by sending seraph serpents to bite them, such that many of them died! Yet we see how God used this to turn the people back to him, as they renewed their faith in God. The solution of looking at a bronze seraph serpent on a pole for healing is such a powerful symbol that it has become a standard icon for the medical profession.

Perhaps more importantly, this healing is seen as a prefiguring of Jesus' death on the cross. For it is when we look up to the cross, with Jesus in the act of offering his life for our sins, that we find authentic healing. Looking to the seraph serpent brought physical healing from a snake bite and the supernatural healing of turning back to God. This is even more true when we look up to Christ on the cross and review our lives through all the many blessings God has given us. The realization of God's providence in our lives thus far helps us to unite our sufferings now. With such a supernatural perspective, we will grow in gratitude, finding greater patience for the journey, with the assurance that God's providence will continue.

**Pray**

To attend to the groaning of the prisoners, to release those doomed to die. (Psalm 102:21)

## Ponder

- When have I felt my patience worn out by the journey? What circumstances combine to make my life and duties as a parent seem difficult? Do I complain against God for these sufferings?
- How have I lost a supernatural perspective when it comes to the challenges of parenting? Have I taken time to reflect on God's grace throughout my past, thanking him for his kindness and looking to the future with hope?
- How can I look to the cross for healing from my suffering? How can I unite my difficulties to the passion and death of Christ? How might I find resurrection in doing this?

## Do

*This Week: Offering Suffering*

Sometimes we are simply overwhelmed by all that we have to do and the circumstances that make it impossible to do everything as well as we would like. Rather than allowing impatience and resentment to take root, however, we can offer today's challenges to God, trusting that he might be allowing such difficulties in order to help us depend more fully on him.

---

# WEDNESDAY

## Read

- Daniel 3:14–20, 91–92, 95
- Daniel 3:52, 53, 54, 55, 56
  R. Glory and praise for ever!
- John 8:31–42

## Reflect

The story of our first reading from Daniel is an inspiring account of Shadrach, Meshach, and Abednego, standing strong against King Nebuchadnezzar's demand to worship a statue. The three would rather go willingly to their death than commit a sin of idolatry. This account, and many of the stories from the martyrs who refused to pay tribute to false gods, witness to the willingness to endure any suffering out of love for and faithfulness to God.

We might note that few, if any of us, will find ourselves in such a dramatic situation regarding actual idols and false gods. And yet, there are still two worthwhile messages for us in such a passage. First of all, Shadrach, Meshach, and Abednego didn't simply wake up one day with courage to stand strong in their faith; they lived virtuous lives as a result of consistent effort. Many early Christian martyrs embraced asceticism as a way to prepare for imprisonment, torture, and death. While we may not ever be faced with such a stark decision to refuse idolatry, we are faced daily with smaller temptations to change our priorities, putting our faith on the back burner and forsaking Christ in little ways. One small decision or venial sin may seem insignificant in a larger picture, but, in fact, everything matters.

This realization that everything matters should not lead us to scrupulosity (over-scrutinizing each of our thoughts and actions) or despair. Rather, the point is to recognize that the actions of Shadrach, Meshach, and Abednego are the culmination of their virtue. No doubt these three were not sinless, and like us they sometimes failed in prioritizing God. But they also knew their faith and practiced it, such that they were prepared when the moment of the test arrived.

Secondly, we see that God's response to their fidelity is his own fidelity. God saves them from the fire. We know, of course, that God didn't save those early Christian martyrs from their physical death, like in the story from Daniel. Nor was Jesus saved from his physical death. But, in their willingness to be united to the passion and death of Christ, the martyrs found everlasting life.

We may have some fear when it comes to prioritizing God, especially since it will require the embrace of suffering and difficulty. Constant sacrifices of our preferences and comforts are necessary in our lives as parents. We can make such sacrifices bitterly and with resentment, or we can adopt the generosity of God. The tendency toward resentment prevents us from being happy with our situation as parents. But the constant desire and effort to embrace these difficulties and sufferings in order to be united with Christ will allow us to share in his freedom, as described by Jesus in our Gospel reading today.

**Pray**

Blessed are they who have kept the word with a generous heart and yield a harvest through perseverance. (see Luke 8:15)

**Ponder**

- How might it help me to see my little decisions and acts as training, forming me in virtue for bigger challenges?

- How have I experienced God's fidelity to me in my life? When have I felt a loving response or consolation in times of difficulty?
- When have I been generous in my love for my children? Are there particular issues where I need to work on my generosity? How might I avoid bitterness when making sacrifices in the future?

## Do

*This Week: Offering Suffering*

We know that reaching a goal requires sacrifices on our part. The early martyrs made sacrifices to prepare themselves for martyrdom. And while we likely do not have such martyrdom in our future, nonetheless we are called to make sacrifices for our faith in order to strengthen ourselves by uniting us more fully to Christ's suffering on the cross. Today we should think of how we might improve at offering those little parenting challenges as gifts to God.

# THURSDAY

**Read**

- Genesis 17:3–9
- Psalm 105:4–5, 6–7, 8–9
  R. The Lord remembers his covenant for ever.
- John 8:51–59

**Reflect**

Perhaps no other story in the Old Testament is so difficult to read as that of Abraham nearly sacrificing his son Isaac, at the instruction of God. Simplistically, we know this is an account of profound faith in the word of God and willingness to fulfill his word, despite the costs. And yet, most of us find it difficult to imagine actively taking steps with the intention to kill one of our children, even with the clear direction of God.

Thankfully, then, one of the key messages of this story of Abraham and Isaac centers on God's promises and God's actions, rather than the human actors in the story. While Abraham does demonstrate great faith, God's fidelity is even more profound. Even with Abraham's great faith, there is no real equality in such a covenant. Rather, God promises abundance in so many ways and asks for little in return — simply the allegiance he is owed anyway as God.

Abraham is a key figure, however, as we see in today's Gospel passage from John. Those arguing with Jesus object to how Jesus seems to be making himself more important than Abraham. After all, God made a covenant with Abraham! Jesus, of course, intends no disrespect to Abraham — they are on the same team, after all. And that's what the people are failing to realize: Jesus, as God who has become man, is fulfilling the covenant. God's fidelity to his promises to Abraham is Jesus, sitting right there with them.

Those rejecting Jesus here are no worse than the many before them who failed in honoring the covenant. We, too, often act contrary to God's laws, and we too often reject Jesus, even when he is in our midst. Part of the reason for this is our own limited expectations and vision, much like the Jews in conversation with him. Whenever we think we can anticipate how God will work in our lives or the lives of others, we are probably mistaken.

There are times when we want something so badly, even thinking it is best for us, that we pursue it obsessively. Yet our plans, and even our discernment, can lead us astray, such that we cheat ourselves out of what is actually best for us. This is particularly true when it comes to embracing suffering and difficulty. We seldom desire or pursue such challenges, nor do we grasp how important they are for uniting us to Christ. And yet, as we see with Abraham's willingness to sacrifice his son, it is precisely in embracing suffering and difficulty that we are blessed by God. This is believing the word of God, the Word made flesh. We share in Christ's victory over death when we enter into his death.

## Pray

Whoever keeps my word will never see death. (John 8:51)

## Ponder

- How are my expectations limited when it comes to the work of God?
- Have I ever been surprised by events in my life that exceeded what I imagined was possible?
- Has there ever been a time I was sure that something

was the best for me or for my family, but then I was unable to achieve it? Was the result as bad as I feared, or did other good come from it?

**Do**

*This Week: Offering Suffering*

Jesus' words regarding death almost seem ironic when we know the passion and crucifixion that awaits him. And yet, he sees beyond his upcoming death, knowing that it fulfills the covenant and ultimately ends in his resurrection. We, too, need to see beyond our suffering, keeping in mind the final end of eternal life with God. As we strive to offer our suffering to God today, we can remind ourselves that our earthly difficulties are temporary, and are meant to lead us to eternal joy.

# FRIDAY

## Read

- Jeremiah 20:10–13
- Psalm 18:2–3A, 3BC–4, 5–6, 7
  R. In my distress I called upon the Lord, and he heard my voice.
- John 10:31–42

## Reflect

Sometimes, in the midst of the penitential season of Lent, we lose sight of the virtue of hope. Especially when long winter months seem to drag on, with nothing to celebrate and no visible signs of spring, we can begin to despair. Our Lenten resolutions can sometimes even add to the negativity we feel.

In the first reading from the prophet Jeremiah, we have a wonderful illustration of hope, rooted in the confidence of God's strength and intention to save those who believe in him. Jeremiah recognizes the evil intent of those around him, wanting to trap him. And these words also prefigure the person of Jesus, who similarly is targeted for sabotage.

Although we are bound to encounter criticism for how we live our lives, we are unlikely to encounter the attacks described by Jeremiah. Nonetheless, we need to be able to share in the hope expressed in the responsorial psalm and by the prophet. When we are in distress, we should call on the Lord, who is our strength. As winter and Lent drag on, and our everyday difficulties continue, use these occasions to call out to God.

As parents, we often find ourselves in unpleasant or difficult situations. We may not always be able to bear such burdens of life with cheerfulness and smiles, and that is perfectly ok. Dutiful resignation also bespeaks commitment to God's will. But real growth comes not so much in the acceptance of struggles, as in the calling out to God in a spirit of hope, trusting in his help. Of course, we may not always feel confidence in our problems being solved in the way we want. We might not be able even to grasp exactly how God will meet us in the midst of challenges. But hope is fundamentally about habits, not feelings; we can choose to practice the virtue by acknowledging our distress and calling out to God, using the confident words of Psalm 18: "In my distress I called upon the Lord, and he heard my voice."

## Pray

I love you, LORD, my strength. (Psalm 18:2)

## Ponder

- In what specific ways have I been practicing hope in the midst of Lent? As I near the end of Lent, are my resolutions and penances beginning to drag me down or continuing to nourish me? How can I renew my love for Jesus as motivation in these resolutions?
- Was there a time that I anticipated a challenge or difficulty and then found myself better able to respond to it cheerfully? How can changing my expectations prepare me for difficulty and receiving the blessings they might bring?
- When have I called out to God in times of distress? Do I express confidence in his help when I am struggling? Am I growing closer to God through my daily experience of parenting?

## Do

*This Week: Offering Suffering*

Today, let us focus on the important aspect of crying out to God in distress. Many figures in our faith have done precisely that, complaining to God or lamenting their troubles. The willingness to cry out to God indicates our faith in his love and mercy, as well as God's loving concern for us in our unique situations and personal challenges. When we offer our sufferings to God, we are crying out to him in a very real way. In the confidence brought by hope, we thus can let the struggles of parenting lead us to greater dependence upon God.

# SATURDAY

**Read**

- Ezekiel 37:21–28
- Jeremiah 31:10, 11–12ABCD, 13
  R. The Lord will guard us, as a shepherd guards his flock.
- John 11:45–56

**Reflect**

As parents, one of the hardest challenges we may encounter is having to watch our children make mistakes. Even though we know that this is simply a part of life, it is never easy to watch them struggle. When they are young, we can make efforts to start training ourselves to let them make mistakes and learn from them! Of course, we want to encourage a sporting spirit, a willingness to get back up after falling down, to try again to tie the shoestrings after days of not getting it, to retake that class they failed. But we also need optimism and perseverance, learning to see a bigger picture as we watch our children struggle, even if they don't finally succeed in the way we want them to. Furthermore, we need to recognize that our will for them is not always God's will for them, and sometimes their decisions, even when we judge them to be mistakes, result in them growing closer to God.

Although God is above the human sort of "feelings" associated with such a parenting struggle, we can witness the profound love that is his essence. This great love of God is expressed in our first reading from Ezekiel. It is not so much that God is "hurt" by idolatry and apostasy, the sins and failings of the people Israel. Rather, like a good parent, God wants what is best for his children! And God knows what is best: the unity of the people who worship God and follow his commands out of love for him.

As parents, we know that there's nothing easy about this. Even when we clearly see what is best for our children and communicate that to them, they often choose to do the opposite of our counsel, seemingly wanting to experience the consequences firsthand, rather than to be saved from them. It's no wonder that we want to step in, to interfere with their decisions, and to save them from the results of their mistakes. Sometimes, we need to guide children to find a way out of their mess. While respecting their freedom, we also want them to maintain a sense of hope, rather than falling into despair. And so we also need to maintain our hope.

It's beautiful, then, that the Old Testament provides us with many accounts of the failings of the people of Israel, coupled with God's efforts to bring them back to himself. God's willingness to establish covenants and his faithfulness to them despite the people's sins exemplifies the love God has for us. Paradigmatically, this love for us is expressed in the Incarnation: God-made-man in the body of Mary, born for us in Bethlehem. And this love incarnate reaches a culmination in the passion and death of Christ, followed by his resurrection from the dead. Even after the many mistakes of his people, we see that God continues to provide generously for us all, including us in our weaknesses and our children in theirs.

As we prepare to enter Holy Week, we might reflect upon that love of God, who did not want us to despair, drowning in the mess of our own sins with no way out. Instead of forcing our obedience or abandoning us in misery, God saves us from the mess through his own action. As human parents, we know this is not always possible. But as children of God, we recognize that this is everything to us. Responding to this abundant love with our own love and gratitude is always our task, and particularly as we begin Holy Week, we must keep this in mind.

## Pray

I will be their God, and they will be my people. (Ezekiel 37:27)

## Ponder

- How have I witnessed my children making mistakes? How have I worked on training myself to let them learn from consequences?
- How have I found comfort in God's mercy through my willingness to confess my sins? How do I recognize God's stepping in to save me from my mess?
- How do I respond to God's abundant love? How do I communicate this in the context of family, especially to my children?

## Do

*This Week: Offering Suffering*

It's hard to watch children fail. Just as we don't really desire it for our children, God does not want it for us. Nonetheless, God does allow suffering, and that is because it represents a great opportunity for us. As we continue to offer our suffering this week, let us try doing so in a way that acknowledges how we are actually benefiting from the practice, particularly in growing closer to God during this season of Lent.

# HOLY WEEK AND EASTER

*Sharing in the Life and Death of Jesus*

---

# PALM SUNDAY OF THE LORD'S PASSION

## Read

At the Procession with Palms

- Matthew 21:1–11

At the Mass

- Isaiah 50:4–7
- Psalm 22:8–9, 17–18, 19–20, 23–24

  R. My God, my God, why have you abandoned me?
- Philippians 2:6–11
- Matthew 26:14–27:66

## Reflect

Our readings for today are longer than usual and capture so much of what all of Lent, and all of our Christian life, concerns. In the Gospel at the blessing of palms, we hear of the welcome Jesus found as he entered the city of Jerusalem; then, in an abrupt switch, the Gospel at Mass tells of his rejection, passion, and crucifixion. Here we find the tension between believing in Christ, our Lord and Messiah, and our tendency to refuse him the place he deserves in our lives.

As we begin this final week before our Easter celebration, we are asked to enter into Jesus' passion, recognizing the power of love represented by his willingness to undergo his passion and death. All of our Lent should have been preparing us to enter into these mysteries of Holy Week; but if we do not feel prepared, or have felt overwhelmed by various responsibilities and other distractions throughout Lent, it is not too late to share in Christ's journey.

We often feel as though everything depends upon us. Indeed, this is especially true of family life because, in fact, so much does depend upon us! We are responsible for providing food, clothing, and shelter for our children, not to mention love, affirmation, education, and faith formation. We are constantly reminded that our behavior is modeling for our children, and possibly the most important influence they have is our example. The pressures can be so overwhelming!

This week, however, we are reminded that everything actually depends upon Christ, and not ourselves. Ultimately our salvation, and that of our children, is not something we earn by avoiding sin and living virtuously. Nor do we earn the celebration of Easter by completing five-star Lenten resolutions. Rather, Holy Week is about entering into the mysteries of our faith, sharing in the passion and death of Christ, and recognizing that we are not finally in charge of everything that happens, even with regard to our children.

Far from leading us to despair, this realization brings courage, and even joyful optimism. We are almost to the conclusion of Lent, and we know that Easter awaits us. During this week, we will still have work to do around the house, and we will need to care for our children as usual. Let's turn our focus to Christ as we do these tasks knowing that whatever the pressures we feel, we are given a great gift in his embrace of the cross.

## Pray

He humbled himself, becoming obedient to death, even death on a cross. (Philippians 2:8)

## Ponder

- How do I both welcome and reject Christ? When have I fallen short in this year's journey of Lent? How can I let my failures be a cause for courage rather than despair?

- Do I sometimes act as though everything depends upon me? Do I feel this pressure and make it evident to my family? How do I keep in mind Christ's final victory?
- How can I be recollected this week, focusing my attention on Christ's passion and death?

**Do**

*Stations of the Cross: 1) Jesus is condemned to death; 2) Jesus embraces his cross*

Today, take some time to reflect on the first two stations of the cross. There is so much injustice in the world that it can seem overwhelming at times. We should make efforts to remedy injustice, but we also look to Jesus' acceptance of his condemnation when we encounter many difficulties that seem unfair and feel like heavy burdens. At such times, we unite our sufferings to Christ. Whether we say Jesus "embraces" his cross or "takes up his cross," we clearly see his intent and purposefulness as this final journey begins. Jesus tells us that we must take up our cross and follow him if we want to be his disciples. Our daily burdens are a participation in this journey. Our crosses are real crosses, and they become meaningful and valuable when we join them to Christ.

# MONDAY OF HOLY WEEK

## Read

- Isaiah 42:1–7
- Psalm 27:1, 2, 3, 13–14
  R. The Lord is my light and my salvation.
- John 12:1–11

## Reflect

When we hear this story from the Gospel passage of Mary anointing Jesus' feet, we can see how some, not just Judas Iscariot, would view it as a lavish waste. Judas describes it as being worth "three hundred days' wages," and thus Mary likely undertook great sacrifice to procure it. Jesus, however, does not seem to view it as a waste, and he does not fault Mary's intention. Instead, he relates her anointing to his burial, which reveals a profound connection when it comes to such ideas of "waste."

The truth is that no attention, no commitment, no time, no love, no resources, are ever wasted when they are spent on Jesus. Here is God made man, our Lord and Messiah. There is simply no way to do too much when it comes to worshipping and honoring Jesus. And this story implies that those who question this truth might have ulterior motives for their criticism.

If Mary's use of costly oil to anoint Jesus could appear wasteful, so also could Jesus' very death seem wasteful. Mary, at least, uses this oil to anoint the feet of the Incarnate God, hearkening back to the wise men's gifts, especially myrrh, to the child Jesus. Jesus' generosity can seem even more truly wasteful; he spends his life and even offers his death for us who are mere humans, deserving of nothing. God makes his dwelling among us, bearing the ordinary burdens of life and work on earth, and encountering even more extraordinary struggles with the constant rejection of those who should welcome God in their midst. And when that final persecution and passion comes, he does not return the rejection, but rather embraces the cross, moving forward in the journey to his death.

What a beautiful gift and generous sacrifice of God! And perhaps somewhat surprisingly, God does not seem to see this as wasteful at all. He deems it worthwhile and fulfills the covenant promises to his people through his very self, in the flesh, in Jesus. There is no bitterness or resentment, just abundant love. God is the prodigal, or wasteful, father, who spares nothing to save his people from their sins.

The sacrifices of parenting pale in comparison, perhaps. Yet, we might sometimes hear the perspective of others who see us as having "wasted" our time, money, attention, careers, etc. for our children. We could be wearing expensive clothing with neatly ordered lives and impressive jobs, winning recognition from many, as well as the compensation of seven-figure salaries. We could take luxurious vacations twice a year, excel at some amazing hobby, or at least get eight hours of sleep each night and have time to binge-watch Netflix. Instead, we find ourselves mopping up spilled milk, spending hours at the emergency room to get X-rays on a broken arm, folding laundry at 9:00 p.m., and trying to organize a weekend that involves soccer games, birthday parties, music lessons, and more.

What a waste! And yet, when we are committed to our families, and, more importantly, committed to living the Christian life, we can't see any waste in this at all. Every act — no matter how mundane or difficult — can become a way of worshipping Jesus, anointing his feet to prepare for his burial. We can never pay back to him the debt that we owe, but we also know that he doesn't expect us to do so. Rather, he invites us to share in his life, with all the burdens, and to offer to him everything we have.

## Pray

You alone are compassionate with our faults.

## Ponder

- How do I choose to "waste" my time on Jesus in ways that others cannot understand?
- Have I been told that I've "wasted" my life on children? How does that make me feel? If I respond to this limited understanding, how do I respond?
- How can I cultivate gratitude for the opportunity to "waste" my time on others in a way that also honors Christ?

## Do

*Stations of the Cross: 3) Jesus falls the first time; 4) Jesus meets his blessed mother*

Today, take some time to reflect on the third and fourth stations of the cross. This trek to his death is hard for Jesus, having already undergone scourging and other mistreatment. In a display of humanity, Jesus falls this first time. As parents, we know that life involves struggle and failure. Yet, the falls remind us of our weakness and need for God to help us through the difficulties in life in order to continue our journey. We also see Mary's support for her son that continues now even in the hour of his passion. We are often called to this painful role of supporting our children in times of difficulty, and we must pray for our readiness to share their suffering, demonstrating compassion, and reminding them through our presence that even in the midst of such struggles and our own pain, we will never abandon them.

# TUESDAY OF HOLY WEEK

**Read**

- Isaiah 49:1–6
- Psalm 71:1–2, 3–4A, 5AB–6AB, 15, and 17
  R. I will sing of your salvation.
- John 13:21–33, 36–38

**Reflect**

Betrayal. We might say it is the theme of today's Gospel passage from John. Jesus is celebrating his final Passover meal, known as the Last Supper, and he is surrounded by twelve of his closest friends. Among them is Judas Iscariot, who will hand him over to authorities for a sum of silver. Also among them is Peter, who denies any association with Jesus three times at the time of his trial. We might think that Jesus, as God, is above being bothered by such human infidelity. Yet, the passage begins by noting that Jesus was deeply troubled (see Jn 13:21).

If you've ever experienced betrayal, then you know how deeply troubling it is — in part because it is so unexpected, and even more so because it is so unjust. When we have been a faithful friend to the point of sacrifice, it can be hard to imagine someone else would take this fidelity for granted.

And yet, the Gospel passage today seems right in line with much of the Old Testament stories. God remains faithful to his people, who turn to idols, betraying God for selfish interests and false gods of other nations. That his own disciples would betray Jesus appears as a continuation of these infidelities of the people. And once again, we find that the lack of faithfulness of the people is met by God's own fidelity. In this Last Supper, Jesus gives us the Eucharist, his Body and Blood. With his passion and death looming, we are presented with Jesus' continued presence among his people in the Eucharist.

Where do we fit in this story? We may not see ourselves as Judas, who would hand Jesus over to his death. We may regard ourselves in the place of John, the beloved disciple, who is faithful throughout the passion and with Mary as Jesus hangs on the cross. More likely, however, we can see ourselves in the place of Peter; we want and intend to be faithful, yet somehow we repeatedly fail the test. When we are faced with difficulty, we take the easy way, returning to selfish inclinations. This happens both in our relationships with others and in our relationship with Jesus. Of course, as we see in the life of Peter, reconciliation is possible. Our failures in relationships with friends and family can bring a powerful invitation for humility. We know there have been times we mistakenly assumed the worst interpretation of someone's actions and possibly even criticized them to others. At other times, we may neglect a relationship in a way that is hurtful to the person. Or maybe we have been at the receiving end of this kind of injustice, feeling like we can't do anything right and are constantly being misjudged. We easily hold onto resentment, finding it difficult to forgive.

These challenges in relationships deserve our attention, and we can look to Jesus, celebrating the Passover meal with Judas and Peter. Although Jesus is troubled, he remains faithful and steady to the course of his passion and death. He continues loving Peter and Judas, despite their betrayals. There is no better friend than Jesus. Especially in the difficult seasons of parenting, it can be hard to maintain friendships that sustain us through our unique trials. Let us remember, then, that Jesus is always there for us. He desires our fidelity and is troubled at our betrayals, but he is also willing to take us back, and Jesus himself is our means of reconciliation and healing. His death brings ultimate victory in the

Resurrection, and our sharing in that death brings us to new life.

**Pray**

Be my rock of refuge, my stronghold to give me safety. (Psalm 71:3)

**Ponder**

- How have I been like Peter, intending to be faithful, but falling short in my resolve? Do I regularly seek reconciliation with Jesus in the Sacrament of Confession, as well as with those I have betrayed?
- How can I improve my understanding that Jesus is my ever-faithful friend? How does he show his friendship with me? How can I improve my own fidelity to that friendship?
- How is Jesus a model for prayer? How do I reflect on his model in improving my own prayer life?

**Do**

*Stations of the Cross: 5) Simon helps Jesus carry the cross; 6) Veronica wipes the face of Jesus*

Today, take some time to reflect on the fifth and sixth stations of the cross. The task set upon Jesus is so difficult for him in his already weakened state that he won't be able to carry this burden alone. This is so true for us with so many of our daily crosses as parents; they are too much for us to bear on our own. And sometimes we feel that there is nothing we can do to help others, including our own children. We cannot take up and carry others' crosses to the end; even Simon gave Jesus' cross back to him. But we can still be present and minister to those in need, rather than avoiding them. Veronica's act may seem small, but it was done with great love. As parents, we look to these opportunities to demonstrate love and concern, even when we cannot take away our children's problems. Let us pray for the wisdom and the strength to recognize when we need help and to seek out that help, and let us also pray that we might be able to help those around us who are in need.

# WEDNESDAY OF HOLY WEEK

## Read

- Isaiah 50:4–9A
- Psalm 69:8–10, 21–22, 31, and 33–34
  R. Lord, in your great love, answer me.
- Matthew 26:14–25

## Reflect

It is hard to imagine having a will perfectly in tune with God's. Much of our daily life consists in wanting to go about our own way and running up against obstacles to our plans. This is even true when we want to do God's will and think we are trying to do it. I recently planned to attend the funeral of a neighbor's father and was about to step out the door when my son fell, cutting his head and requiring staples at urgent care! Because of our many ambitions, goals, and more selfish desires as well as our best intentions, we often find it hard to react to the obstacles that come our way.

As we seek to share in the life and death of Jesus during this Holy Week, it is helpful to consider how Jesus responded to his own trials. With a will that was completely in line with his Father's, he was able to bear burdens gracefully, to accept them without complaint despite his distress.

The first reading from Isaiah is a beautiful depiction of this, prefiguring Jesus' perspective in these days leading up to his crucifixion. In this passage we see an awareness of God's gifts, a willingness to use them for others, and dependence upon and trust in God that enables the speaker to accept the unjust criticism, persecution, and abuse of others.

We see this also in Jesus as he sits at the table with the Twelve. He knows that Judas has betrayed him. And yet, he doesn't seek to avoid the traumatic events to come. He allows events to take their course, knowing it to be the will of the Father and the way that God will save his people.

Imagine if we were to live our lives in this way! If we sought to see God's will in all the troubles and inconveniences that came our way, what would our lives be like? How would it change our parenting if we truly trusted in and depended upon God at every moment, seeking to align our will to his? A newfound flexibility in dealing with challenges would surely be a powerful witness to our children and others around us — even more so if we were able to maintain a peaceful demeanor fitting to genuine belief in God's providence in every circumstance. As we share in the life and death of Jesus during this Holy Week, let us reflect on how we can imitate Christ in his faithful response to the trials he endures.

## Pray

God, in your abundant kindness, answer me. (Psalm 69:14C)

## Ponder

- What was a time when I felt my will to be much different from that of God's? Looking back, how did that disparity cause or heighten my stress, disappointment, or anger?
- Do I make efforts to be peaceful in responding to challenges? How do my children learn from me positive ways to react to difficulties?
- How often do I recall throughout my day that I am a part of something bigger than myself? Do I allow this larger narrative to bring me some comfort and peace?

**Do**

*Stations of the Cross: 7) Jesus falls the second time; 8) Jesus meets the women of Jerusalem*

Today, take some time to reflect on the seventh and eighth stations of the cross. Falling is part of human life, and so is falling again. Getting up the second time requires a certain resignation for the task and a strong desire to persevere to the end. This path that Jesus walks is difficult; the weight of the wood is heavy. Jesus does not reject this burden, however, but gives us an example of perseverance that we must choose to follow since we have chosen to be his disciples. Jesus' words to the women — "Do not weep for me; weep instead for yourselves and for your children" (Lk 23:28) — seem to be a warning to them of the calamities ahead. Jesus' resurrection is the victory over death, but it does not remove difficulty from the world. How beautiful that Jesus can speak to these women from the midst of his pain, demonstrating concern for their suffering! This is our Savior, who loves us and cares for us, who shares in our troubles all the more when we pick up our crosses again and unite them to his own.

---

# HOLY THURSDAY — EVENING MASS OF THE LORD'S SUPPER

## Read

- Exodus 12:1–8, 11–14
- Psalm 116:12–13, 15–16BC, 17–18
  R. Our blessing-cup is a communion with the Blood of Christ.
- 1 Corinthians 11:23–26
- John 13:1–15

## Reflect

Lent is a long season. But today, on Holy Thursday, you've made it! We are finally here, at the Holy Triduum, in the final days leading up to Easter Sunday. Holy Thursday is a beautiful beginning to this, because it does not have the same penitential feel as the Lenten days preceding it. Today we commemorate and reflect upon various gifts we have received from Christ: first and foremost, the Eucharist; secondly, the priesthood, which is instituted at this Last Supper and allows for the daily consecration and celebration of the Eucharist; and thirdly, the model of Christian service that we see demonstrated by Jesus as he washes the feet of his disciples.

Let's begin with the third of these for our reflections today, since, as parents, we probably have some practice with washing feet (and little bodies). In the barefoot days of summer, while washing my little one's feet, I will sometimes mention, "You know, Jesus washed the feet of his disciples." And while this act was symbolic, setting a model that goes far beyond the details of dirty feet and clean water, nonetheless, it was also real, just as real as when we help out our children in the tub or rinse them down with the backyard hose.

We sometimes overlook this privilege that we have as parents. We are given so many opportunities to minister to our children, in imitation of Christ's own service. There are corporal and spiritual works of mercy identified by the Church, including feeding the hungry, clothing the naked, caring for the sick, admonishing sinners, forgiving offenses, and instructing the ignorant. For some, these works of mercy may take planning and effort. People have to seek out opportunities to help others in this way, perhaps by visiting a nursing home or donating to a homeless shelter. As parents, however, we find these acts are simply part of our lives. Every single day we have such opportunities to live these works of mercy, inspired by the service of Jesus.

Family life is a different way of living the Faith than that of a professed religious living in a convent or monastery, and it is a different way of living the Faith than our young, single days, when we had time for hours of Eucharistic adoration or volunteering in various parish ministries. But while our faith life now may feel limited in time for prayer, we are reminded today how much the Church values service to others. For all those times when we have despaired of having the prayer life we felt necessary, let us remember that our faith led us to be open to the children we've welcomed into our home. And it is also our faith that sustains us in caring for our family.

But the other aspects of Holy Thursday are important, too: the Eucharist and the priesthood. We are on the same team as our priests, though we sometimes forget that, and the whole Body of Christ is united and strengthened through this gift of the Eucharist. While priests are easily criticized today, and the Church has certainly suffered from men who have abused their role in the Church, many of us have also benefited greatly from the service of priests — those who have baptized us, given us Communion, heard our confessions, inspired us with their faith, comforted us with their compassion at the time of a family member's death, etc. Despite those who have given the priesthood a bad name, there are many holy men who have undertaken ordination and priestly service with good motivation and holy intent. We are grateful for such a gift of priests who also imitate Christ in their service.

The Eucharist is such an amazing gift. It is the Body and Blood of Christ given for us, nourishing and strengthening us so we can live this Christian life on earth. The whole Church is united in this sacrament, which is the rightful focus of every Mass that we celebrate on each day throughout the year. Today, we are particularly mindful of the sustenance we receive. Christ has become our Passover lamb, offering his own Body and Blood, for us. And he calls us to share in this sacrifice. He does not demand our obedience and service, expecting us to live as he did with no assistance. Rather, he invites us to imitate him, but he makes that love and generosity possible by nourishing us with the Eucharist.

## Pray

This is my body that is for you. (1 Corinthians 11:24)

## Ponder

- Have I ever experienced others demeaning the life of service that comes with parenting? What was my response then? What would my response be now?
- Are there some mundane household chores I dislike that might be beneficial to think of in terms of following Jesus' model?
- Am I focused as I begin this Triduum? How can I recollect myself during these days to stay focused on the events the Church is commemorating?

**Do**

*Stations of the Cross: 9) Jesus falls the third time; 10) Jesus is stripped of his garments*

Today, take some time to reflect on the ninth and tenth stations of the cross. As he nears Golgotha where he will be crucified, Jesus has come to the end of his strength; he simply cannot go farther. He has struggled to finish his trek, and his death is near. But first, insult is added to Jesus' many injuries. To the physical pain is added the humiliation of nakedness, demonstrating Jesus' complete vulnerability. There are times when we feel we can go no farther, even feeling vulnerable and humiliated in front of others. And yet, we can imitate Christ in the midst of such pain. If we let our vulnerability become a sharing in his own, we will find new strength in our dependence upon him. With circumstances so out of his control, there is nothing left for Jesus but complete trust and dependence upon his loving Father. Let us pray that when we feel ourselves in desperate circumstances, we will think of Jesus at this moment and choose to rely fully on God.

# GOOD FRIDAY OF THE LORD'S PASSION

## *Obligatory day of fast and abstinence*

**Read**

- Isaiah 52:13—53:12
- Psalm 31:2, 6, 12–13, 15–16, 17, 25
  R. Father, into your hands I commend my spirit.
- Hebrews 4:14–16; 5:7–9
- John 18:1—19:42

**Reflect**

We have come to Good Friday of the Lord's Passion, the day when we commemorate Jesus' sufferings and crucifixion. Today is the only day in the calendar year when no Mass is celebrated. There is no consecration during today's afternoon service; rather, the Eucharist we consume today was reserved from yesterday's Holy Thursday Mass. We hear the passion of Jesus from the Gospel of John, and we pray for various groups of people, especially those who do not share our faith. Moreover, today is a day of both fast and abstinence. And today is usually a day off from school, so we most likely have our children with us. Given all these factors, Good Friday can feel very difficult for parents. We want to maintain a somewhat somber atmosphere in the home to help our children realize the importance of the day. But we also want to avoid being angry and losing our patience as the result of a long, challenging Church service and the demands of fasting.

Perhaps we can keep these goals in perspective when we maintain our own focus on Christ. It is wonderful to have family practices to mark the day as unique and even penitential, and if we can help our children grow in appreciation for Christ's sacrifice on the cross, we will be forming them well in the Faith. However, this day is not ultimately about us or the difficulties and challenges of this particular day for parents.

We can truly share in Jesus' passion on this day. There is a certain docility described in the "Suffering Servant" passage from Isaiah in our first reading today. And as we hear the passion account of Jesus' death and crucifixion, Jesus can appear somewhat passive through it all. That passivity or docility, however, is but the surface appearance of a determined will. It may seem as though everything is out of his control; but, in another sense, everything is completely under his control. Jesus is one with the Father; Jesus' human and divine wills are perfectly aligned. Jesus is doing exactly what he intended to do in bearing the burden of the cross and accepting his crucifixion.

If we want to live Good Friday well, and the Christian life in general well, we should adopt this perspective of Christ. Even in the face of difficulty, we can respond with steely determination. Motivated by love, we can attend to our commitments and responsibilities as parents. We can, like Jesus, do what we must do, with an external appearance of passivity or docility. Answering children's requests with a smile rather than a complaint may come easily for some and be harder for others. But our efforts to imitate Christ, especially on this day, should be felt by us, even if not identified by others.

## Pray

Yet it was our pain that he bore, our sufferings he endured. (Isaiah 53:4)

## Ponder

- What can I do today in my home to mark Good Friday as a day different from others, and maintain a peaceful, perhaps somber, atmosphere?
- What challenges have I undertaken with an appearance of passivity, yet relying upon an underlying determined will, like Christ accepting his passion? How did my determination help me to get through something so difficult?
- Am I looking forward to the Resurrection and the celebration of Easter Sunday? How can I keep this final end in mind today as I reflect on Jesus' passion and death?

## Do

*Stations of the Cross: 11) Jesus is nailed to the cross; 12) Jesus dies on the cross*

Today, take some time to reflect on the eleventh and twelfth stations of the cross. Here is that most painful and profound moment for all of us who call ourselves Christian. Jesus is nailed to the cross in an unjust and inhumane act, laying down his own life to save all of us who deserve death and judgment for our sins. In the midst of our own troubles and challenges, we sometimes lose sight of Christ on the cross. We put ourselves in the center of the narrative where Jesus' crucifixion should be, failing to recognize that our problems become more meaningful when we allow them to lead us to Christ, and Christ on the cross, rather than turning us back upon ourselves. Jesus, God made man, who dwelt among us, dies like any other human — the last breath, the last beat of his heart, the last movement of his limbs, until he hangs in stillness. The world, however, will never be the same. We cannot be the same; we want to be transformed by this ultimate gift of self, the sacrifice made willingly out of love for us. We will strive to live our lives in cruciform, giving of ourselves willingly out of love for Christ.

# HOLY SATURDAY

**Read**

Our Mass readings for today are from the Easter Vigil service; no daytime Masses are celebrated today. These readings are not included here due to their number.

**Reflect**

If you are able to attend the vigil, you will note the beautiful readings conveying all of salvation history throughout the Old Testament, culminating in the death and resurrection of Christ. There are so many of these readings that parishes often select from among them, and the Easter Vigil services are often the most remarkable and beautiful of the entire year. You may want your children to experience this unique Mass, or you might find it a good night for a babysitter to put your young children to bed while you attend the vigil.

Before this vigil service, however, we have the day of Holy Saturday. Holy Saturday is associated with the Harrowing of Hell, Jesus' descent to the underworld of the dead to proclaim the Good News and bring forth the holy ones who had died. It is also sometimes said that Jesus kept the perfect Sabbath on this day: His body lying in the tomb on this Saturday represents a complete resting in God. And it furthermore resonates with the image of God in the creation story of Genesis, resting on the seventh day after creating the world.

It would be lovely if we, too, could spend this day in a state of rest. We are always so busy, and the lack of rest takes a toll on us. The opportunity to rest shows a trust in the work of God, that not everything is dependent upon our own actions. And rest, furthermore, is a meeting place with God.

But, of course, we still have kids today! And so it is unlikely that we can make this a day of rest where we solely contemplate the silence of the tomb. Rather, we will be recalling Jesus' rest in the tomb as we find ourselves preparing the daily meals and tripping over toys. And that is ok. We can have a good Holy Saturday in the midst of our usual family life, whether we find silence and rest or sacrifice these for the needs of others.

Today is a good day to recognize both the importance and benefit of rest and silence, as well as our generosity in being willing to forgo them for our children if necessary. It is great to keep a low-key family atmosphere today. As parents, today we may be finalizing our children's Easter baskets, ironing Easter clothes, preparing in advance some of our special Easter foods, and maybe even spending time with our children dying Easter eggs. The material aspects mark Easter day as special for our children, and we should embrace our role here. These preparations are part of how we honor Easter Sunday! However, let us keep in mind that the joy of the celebration does not stem from our preparations of these details, but from the resurrection of Christ. It is a gift to share in the joy of the day, just as we shared in the life and death of Jesus.

**Pray**

Save us, Savior of the world.

**Ponder**

- What is striking about the image of Jesus resting in the tomb? Do I ever long for such perfect rest from my work here on earth?
- Do I ever think of my children as detracting from my spiritual experience of important holy days? How can I re-narrate my responsibilities, seeing them in terms of

generous sacrifice that aids my own holiness?

- Do I feel ready for this Easter? Did my Lenten practices and my experience of Holy Thursday and Good Friday prepare me well to share in the joy of Easter?

**Do**

*Stations of the Cross: 13) Jesus is taken down from the cross; 14) Jesus is laid in the tomb*

Today, take some time to reflect on the last two stations of the cross. After the soldier thrusts a lance in his side to make sure he is dead, Jesus is taken down from the cross and placed in the arms of his mother. We can imagine the sorrow of that moment, even if no words can capture the agony of watching a child suffer to the point of such a horrific death. But Mary is faithful through it all; she embraces his body that was once within her own, and she loves him even in his death and placement in the tomb. Like Mary, we maintain our faith, hope, and love. It may seem that the story has come to its finish, but we know that this is a new beginning. From the tomb will come hope and new life, Jesus in his resurrection. With our limited human understanding, we can't always distinguish what is truly the end and what might be a beginning for us or our children. Thus, we pray that we might always cultivate these virtues of faith, hope, and love, believing that God will provide for us what is best for us and our children if we always remain close to Jesus.

# CELEBRATING EASTER

## *Making the Joy Last (at least) an Octave!*

### Read

- Acts 10:34A, 37–43
- Psalm 118:1–2, 16–17, 22–23
- Colossians 3:1–4 or 1 Corinthians 5:6B–8
- John 20:1–9

### Reflect

After that long season of Lent, we may find that Easter seems to come and go too quickly. We spend weeks in preparation, trying to live out our Lenten resolutions and enter into the traditional practices of prayer, fasting, and almsgiving. If we have lived Lent well, we have had many opportunities to grow closer to God in various ways. Now, suddenly, Easter Sunday comes … and goes!

We Catholics, however, celebrate Easter as an octave. Easter Sunday is the highest liturgical feast day in the whole year. And yet, Easter Monday is also a solemnity, the highest rank of feasts in the Church. Easter Tuesday is also a solemnity, and so on, all the way through Divine Mercy Sunday, which ends the octave of Easter. And even then, the Easter season continues! While Lent is a mere forty days (plus Sundays), Easter is fifty days (plus Sundays). So we can see that the celebration of the Resurrection is so important that the Church emphasizes it by extending the day into an octave and into a whole season.

Easter Sunday stands in stark contrast to the days immediately preceding it. Whether we have had a "good" Lent, as we would define it, or a "bad" Lent, Jesus Christ is risen from the dead!

Alleluia, he is risen! We are invited to share in the celebration, whether we think that we were the first invited to the banquet, or the last, called in to fill up the tables. We are furthermore invited to extend this celebration, to continue to rejoice in the victory of Christ. And, as the days of the long Easter season go on, we also begin to turn our attention toward Pentecost, and to prepare ourselves to celebrate the coming of the Holy Spirit.

Yet, in many ways, Lent seems to continue for us parents. Yes, our particular Lenten resolutions have ended. The Church does not call for the same penitential discipline now. But despite this being a season of celebration, rejoicing in the triumph of Christ over death, our own struggles as parents may continue on very much as before. The limitations on our time and schedule, the financial demands, and the constant concerns of how best to raise our children as Catholics in this world, are just as much a part of Easter as of Lent. In many ways, however, such struggles and sacrifices seem more appropriate to Lent. And, honestly, wouldn't it be amazing if they could all just lessen a bit, now that Easter is here?

Given that we have little control over our circumstances, however, we have to find a way to embrace a perspective that can help us get through these days of Easter, in the midst of years that often feel like Lent. It helps to recognize, and embrace, that parenthood is truly a season of Lent in our lives. Older parents are always eager to tell us how quickly it goes, and how those years were really the best of their lives. Their fond reminiscing doesn't always ease our strain during the busy and stressful times of parenting. And yet, just as we found moments of joy in the midst of Lent, we should look for and enjoy the consolations of parenting children: the funny remarks, the warm hugs and wet kisses, the developing talents, the little successes of learning to tie shoes or ride a bicycle, and the bigger successes such as high school and college graduations.

God never desires or delights in our misery. God only wants us to grow closer to himself, and we can do this both in our joys and struggles as parents. If you feel like Lent is continuing for you, even though you should be celebrating Easter, do not despair. Look for the joys and continue to embrace the cross, trusting that God can make of us what he wants if we will depend on him and seek to do his will always.

**Pray**

This is the day the Lord has made. Let us rejoice and be glad!

**Ponder**

- Did this Easter feel different from others? Did I ultimately feel prepared or unprepared for the celebration? How can I still make efforts to celebrate, regardless?
- How can I let the joy of the Resurrection permeate my life? How can I share this joy with my family?
- Am I grateful for Easter? How do I express my gratitude to God for all of my blessings, especially those of family life?

**Do**

As we move into the Easter season, consider finding ways to mark the octave of Easter and the season of Easter as different and special. Here are a few ideas.

- Extend the special foods designated for Easter throughout the octave. Perhaps reserve a chocolate egg for each child to be given on every day of the octave of Easter. Arrange for favorite or special meals throughout the octave. Plan a different dessert for each day of the octave.
- Plan some special day trips for the family throughout the

season of Easter. Look for events that can mark the season as different from the usual daily grind of family life.

- Intentionally try to host friends or family in the Easter season. If the thought of hosting seems overwhelming, plan picnics or park meetups with friends.
- Keep fresh flowers in the house throughout the Easter season.
- Seek out the natural beauty of springtime, if nature cooperates! Look for cherry blossom times, find some blooming gardens, revisit old favorite forest hiking trails to see whether the plants are showing new greenery.
- Have some Easter decorations up on Easter Sunday, but make sure to keep them up at least through the octave of Easter, and possibly longer!
- Pray the Divine Mercy chaplet as a family during the octave of Easter, in preparation for Divine Mercy Sunday.
- Learn the Regina Caeli ("Queen of Heaven, Rejoice") prayer and say it at noon.
- Listen to or sing some traditional Easter hymns.
- Take advantage of Easter candy and Easter decoration clearance sales, and enjoy! Consider doing more than one egg hunt for your children, possibly a week or later into the Easter season.

# APPENDIX

## *Feasts and Solemnities of Lent*

# FEBRUARY 14

## *Memorial of Saints Cyril and Methodius (and Saint Valentine)*

**Read**

Because this is not a high-ranking feast in the Church, you are more likely to hear the regular readings for the day rather than those included here.

- Acts 13:46–49
- Psalm 117:1BC, 2

    R. Go out to all the world and tell the Good News.
- Luke 10:1–9

**Reflect**

Saint feast days are generally rather sparse in Lent; and yet, the saints we commemorate today deserve at least a brief reflection. Cyril and Methodius were brothers of Byzantine Catholicism born in present-day Greece. They were scholars whose linguistic knowledge was reason for them to be sent as missionaries to the Slavic people. Though they frequently found themselves in the midst of political and ecclesial arguments, the two saints ministered to the Slavic people and worked to develop an alphabet for use in translating Scripture to the native language, including for use in the liturgy.

While we don't find Saint Valentine on the liturgical calendar for today, the popularity of Saint Valentine's Day is reason enough to review the traditions surrounding this saint. Saint Valentine is said to be a third-century Christian martyr who was a priest (or possibly a bishop). One miracle associated with him involved the healing of a blind girl, and another story recounts his secretly performing Christian marriage ceremonies, such that the men were able to avoid military conscription. Because these stories are primarily known through legend rather than historical documentation, the Church removed celebration of Saint Valentine's Day from the liturgical calendar, while continuing to acknowledge Saint Valentine as a saint.

The common thread uniting Cyril, Methodius, and Valentine is a love for God and willingness to do God's work despite circumstantial difficulties. Cyril and Methodius did not have an easy time in their work as missionaries among the Slavs, negotiating with Christians of other rites, and they were forced to seek out the assistance of the pope for support in their ministry. And their commitment to the Slavic people and use of their language demonstrates the saints' belief that God's love is for all people. Valentine, similarly a celibate clergyman, lived in a time of Christian persecution, yet did not forsake his faith; rather, he ministered to couples and stood strong in his Christian commitments, to the point of martyrdom.

As parents, it might seem strange to look to the model of celibate men for inspiration during this season of Lent. And yet, we can see here real reason to rely upon Saints Cyril, Methodius, and Valentine. Like these saints, we seek to persevere in doing God's will despite the difficulties. In particular, we recognize the need to help those around us, making sacrifices of our own desires and comforts to facilitate growth in the faith.

By ministering to our children's needs, we already bear witness to our Christian faith. Like Cyril, Methodius, and Valentine, we must be willing to be missionaries in our home, helping to educate our children. In the season of Lent, we have a unique task: to present the penitential discipline of Lent in a positive light. Fasting, abstinence from meat, and our voluntary Lenten resolutions can be difficult for us, and even more so for the children who must put up with us in the meantime! We should guard against these mortifications becoming also mortifications for our children. If we find it difficult to live cheerfully with our voluntarily chosen sacrifices, we may need to reevaluate them in the midst of family life.

If we look to Saints Cyril and Methodius, we do not need to fear mistakes. There may be some steps back, and we may think that our work in raising our children is not bearing and will not bear any fruit. But, as we see with these saints, sometimes the fruit is only evident many years later, even after our deaths. If we remain committed to living the love of God in the midst of family life, we will find, in retrospect, that we truly tried to serve God when we served our children.

## Ponder

- How can I use this Valentine's Day to celebrate the importance of love in my family? Do I help my children with their valentines for friends? How do I communicate my love for my spouse and children today and every day?
- How do I persevere in doing God's will despite the difficulties?
- How do I view my life as participating in the mission of the Church? Do I recognize the missionary impact I can have by being patient, loving, and kind with those who are challenging, within my family and beyond?

## Pray

The harvest is abundant but the laborers are few; so ask the master of the harvest to send out laborers for his harvest. (Luke 10:2)

**Do**

*Giving Valentines*

Many of us already have special ways to celebrate Valentine's Day. It's a great idea especially to write a loving note to our spouses and even our children. We can post brief notes on our kids' doors or find other ways to leave little surprises for our family members.

# FEBRUARY 22

## *Feast of the Chair of Saint Peter, Apostle*

### Read

- 1 Peter 5:1–4
- Psalm 23:1–3A, 4, 5, 6

  R. The Lord is my shepherd; there is nothing I shall want.
- Matthew 16:13–19

### Reflect

Today's feast is a unique one in the Church, celebrating the Chair of Saint Peter, Apostle. We don't normally think of celebrating a chair, and, in fact, beyond the realm of committees and academic departments, we seldom hear the word used for anything other than something upon which to sit.

We already have another feast day to celebrate Saint Peter, listed first among the apostles and understood to be the first of our Catholic popes. This feast of the Chair of Saint Peter is not simply about the person of Peter, a Galilean fisherman. Rather, it is about papal authority and unity, presented to us by this image of the chair. In the context of a committee or an academic department, the chairperson is responsible for coordinating the work of several people. The chair is a communicator, speaking and listening, making decisions, and reporting to others. And while the job of chair is always performed by a person, that person takes on a particular role. In other words, the label of "chair" is not something intrinsic to the person; it can be passed on to another. The very nature of a chair is as a temporary role taken on by someone; but it is crucial, nonetheless, in maintaining unity through leadership.

Although there have been some bad, self-interested popes, as well as controversies about who exactly was the pope and where the real pope should live, this concept of one head of the Church has remained constant since the time of Jesus' death. Nor are these controversies simply of the past; rather, Catholics continue to argue whether the pope is important, how important the pope might be, which documents or statements might be binding, and what would be good reason for dissent from the authority of the pope.

And yet, when we celebrate the Feast of the Chair of Saint Peter, Apostle, we are remembering God's faithfulness to us through the role of the pope, a constant throughout our history. Many empires have come and gone since the beginning of our Church and the reign of Saint Peter as the first pope. Despite all the conflict and controversies now and throughout history, we nonetheless recognize the unity and strength that comes from the Chair of Saint Peter, as well as the endurance of that position. And, as the pope is tasked with facilitating the unity of the Church, we also can powerfully contribute to this unity, through our prayers for the pope and consideration in our speech.

During this season of Lent, we have a great opportunity to use our Lenten resolutions as prayers for others in our Church, as we do penance for our own sins and think how we might, at times, undermine the unity of the Mystical Body of Christ, even within our own homes. Conflict within the Church can be truly painful, as is conflict within the home. In both cases, we might consider the value of forgiving others' faults and prioritizing love and kindness over the desire to be right.

Especially as parents, it can be so difficult to watch our children sin, when we know better and have instructed them in the truth. Our children may not always treat us with the respect we deserve as their parents. They may be unfairly demanding of us at times. Unfortunately, the popes usually encounter worse during their times of service to the Church! So let us be willing to embrace such injustices, responding with love guiding all of our actions, including any necessary corrections we must make in forming our children. And let us use these offenses against us as opportunities to pray for the pope, especially on this Feast of the Chair of Saint Peter.

**Ponder**

- Do I remember to pray for the pope? Do I desire and pray for the unity of the Church?
- How do my actions sometimes bring conflict in the Church? How do my actions foster unity in the Church?
- How does conflict in my family affect me? How does conflict in the Church affect me? Do I turn to God in prayer when concerned about these ruptures?

**Pray**

May all be one! (John 17:21)

**Do**

*Pray an Our Father for the Pope and Unity of the Church*

We know the pain of conflict within the family; the conflict within the Church is also often painful. Today, take a moment simply to offer one Our Father prayer for the pope and his intentions, as well as for the unity of the whole Church under the faithful leadership of the pope.

---

# MARCH 17
## *Memorial of Saint Patrick*

### Read
Today's readings will be the regular Lenten Mass readings, since Saint Patrick's feast day is only observed as a memorial.

### Reflect
Saint Patrick is perhaps one of the most beloved saints for the American people. Although he is the patron saint of Ireland, the large population of Irish Catholics in the United States has helped to spread his fame far beyond Ireland. Everyone wants to be Irish on Saint Patrick's Day! But even if we aren't Irish, we can share his Catholicism, looking to Patrick as a model and asking him to pray for us.

You might not know that Saint Patrick was not born in Ireland. As a young boy, Patrick was kidnapped and taken to Ireland to be sold as a slave. There, he tended animals — spending much time in prayer as he did his duties — until he managed to escape, undertaking the long journey (including hiking and sailing) back to his home in Britain. Reunited with his family, it would seem that all of Patrick's prayers had been answered, and he could live out his days peacefully in his native country.

Yet, Saint Patrick heard God calling him back to Ireland, to go as a missionary priest to convert the pagan peoples that he had lived amongst for so many years. Rather than clinging to comfort, Patrick prepared himself for the journey, gathering supplies and recruiting faithful Catholics who could help him to spread the Gospel in Ireland.

From here, we might be content with a romanticized vision of the Irish people welcoming Patrick and the Christian Faith, making it their own, and settling down in the Irish Catholicism we've come to recognize, employing Gaelic symbols and the shamrock to image the Trinity. But of course, this romanticized picture is far from what actually happened when Patrick returned to Ireland. There he encountered native tribes that tried to kill him, people who converted to the Faith only to massacre their fellow Christians, and overall difficult living conditions that made spreading the Gospel challenging, to say the least.

Saint Patrick might have given up in despair with all that he encountered among the Irish people, but his persistence eventually led to the conversion of all of Ireland. And while Irish Catholics undoubtedly have their own sins and failings like any others in the Church, nonetheless there are many practicing Catholics today who ultimately trace their inherited faith to the work of Saint Patrick in Ireland. The fruit of our good labors is not always known immediately.

On this day when we celebrate Saint Patrick by wearing green and perhaps indulging in Irish (or Irish-American) food and drink, let us also remember the importance of responding to God's call in the midst of adversity. In the context of family life, we are often called — like Patrick — to make great sacrifices of our comfort. When we respond quickly and generously, as he did, we are not guaranteed success or ease, but we are guaranteed the cross, just as he found in his mission to Ireland. And, during this season of Lent, it is precisely a sharing in that cross of Christ that we most desire. We may find that our faithfulness bears fruit in the lives of others, such as our children, who come to share our faith. But even if we never witness such success, we will have done the will of God.

## Ponder

- How do I honor Saint Patrick by making the best from bad situations? When is one instance in my past where I recognize God made something good possible out of something I didn't want?
- Do I ever try to hide my faith? Am I willing to risk the dislike of others in order to share my faith?
- How have I responded to God's calls in the past, even when I knew it would entail difficulty for me? How might I seek to improve my response to God's call in the midst of family life?

## Pray

Christ before me, Christ behind me, Christ in me, Christ with me (see Breastplate of Saint Patrick prayer).

## Do

*Read Saint Patrick's Writings or Prayers*

Many people don't realize that Saint Patrick left behind some beautiful writings and prayers that are easily accessible online. Today, take a moment to look up the Breastplate of Saint Patrick prayer (sometimes called the Lorica of Saint Patrick) or the Confessions of Saint Patrick or Saint Patrick's Letter to Coroticus. If you don't have much time to read today, you can also look up one of the many song versions of Saint Patrick's Breastplate prayer and listen to it.

# MARCH 19

## *Solemnity of Saint Joseph*

**Read**

- 2 Samuel 7:4–5A, 12–14A, 16
- Psalm 89:2–3, 4–5, 27, and 29

  R. The son of David will live forever.
- Romans 4:13, 16–18, 22
- Matthew 1:16, 18–21, 24

**Reflect**

The Solemnity of Saint Joseph comes to us during Lent, providing a special day of celebration in the midst of our usual penances. It may seem strange to celebrate Saint Joseph in the midst of Lent. After all, he is known as the patron saint of a happy death, because it is believed that he was the first to die of the Holy Family, and thus he had Jesus and Mary present with him at his death.

But this means that, unlike Mary, Joseph was not there to witness or share in the adult ministry of Jesus, nor be there to support his son as he was rejected by his people, and ultimately killed. Rather, the little that we know of Saint Joseph comes from the Gospels of Matthew and Luke, who describe Joseph's role at the Nativity and during the early life of Jesus. So we might say that this solemnity turns our thoughts to Christmas!

These thoughts of Joseph in the stable may not seem fitting in the midst of Lent, just as a celebratory solemnity in the midst of Lent may also seem out of place. And yet, this is our faith, and indeed, our life: gift and cross, joy and suffering are often intertwined.

Today's readings show us the significance of Joseph taking on the role of the father of our Lord Jesus, and they also remind us about the known identity of Jesus himself. In the first reading, we hear the promise made to David that he will have a son whose kingdom will last forever. We know that Saint Joseph was in the line of David, as he was required to return to Bethlehem with his family in order to be counted in the census. Thus, Jesus is placed into the line of David, born in Bethlehem, the city of David, and Jesus is the son who fulfills this promise made to David.

Joseph's and Jesus' placement in the line of David is significant for the season of Lent, as much as for Christmas. This is not because being a descendant of David guarantees one's holiness — far from it! Rather, we see that Jesus, known as the son of a righteous man, is also a "son of David," an heir to the Davidic kingdom put in place by God.

Beyond the few stories of the Gospels of Luke and Matthew, not much is known about Saint Joseph. The significance of Joseph may simply be that, like all saints in the Church, Saint Joseph turns our attention to Jesus.

When God became man at the Incarnation, this was no generic act. Rather, Jesus came among us as a baby born to a particular family, whose ancestry was known. But unlike the grandeur associated with David's kingship, Jesus was born in humble circumstances, living out a simple life dedicated to the service of others, and characterized in the end by his suffering and death. Joseph helped to make all of this possible, by ensuring the safety of Jesus' birth, protecting him from Herod by fleeing to Egypt, and raising him for so many years as his own son in the Jewish faith.

As parents, we share the mission of Joseph: to protect and raise our children to live out service to God. Like Joseph, our calling requires difficulty and sacrifices. We may have to change our plans, putting the needs of our children first, as he did. And, like

Joseph, we may not live to see what becomes of them. Nonetheless, if we embrace the challenges, striving to do God's will, we will have done what we were meant to do.

## Ponder

- How does Joseph turn my attention to Jesus? Would my children or friends think that I, too, turn their attention to Jesus?
- How have I put the needs of my children before my own desires and ambitions? Do I ever begrudge those sacrifices, or do I see them in the context of serving God and doing his will?
- What unexpected difficulties have I found most challenging as a parent? Have I learned from them? Have I grown closer to God from these difficulties?

## Pray

His dynasty will continue forever. (Psalm 89:37)

## Do

*Today: Call on Saint Joseph*

Saint Joseph was such a faithful man, dutifully serving Jesus and Mary in his own home. His whole life was dedicated to their well-being and protection. We, too, want to be a part of that household characterized by love and service. Today, let us pray to Saint Joseph throughout the day, asking for his help and guidance to be a good parent, particularly by having a heart open to Jesus.

# MARCH 25

## *Solemnity of the Annunciation*

### Read

- Isaiah 7:10–14; 8:10
- Psalm 40:7–8A, 8B-9, 10, 11
  R. Here I am, Lord; I come to do your will.
- Hebrews 10:4–10
- Luke 1:26–38

### Reflect

It is a beautiful hallmark of our liturgical calendar that this celebration of the Annunciation generally falls in the midst of Lent. The Annunciation celebrates the angel Gabriel announcing to Mary that she would conceive and bear the Son of God by the power of the Holy Spirit. In other words, we are just nine months away from Christmas!

At Christmas we celebrate the Nativity of Christ, his birth in a stable in Bethlehem. And yet, more basically, we also celebrate his Incarnation, that God was made man and dwelt among us. Thus, on this day of the Annunciation, we also celebrate the Incarnation, for this day is both about Mary's yes and Jesus' conception, the beginning of God made flesh dwelling among us.

During Lent, our attention has been turned upon the adult Jesus, the man who walked with his people, challenging them and healing them. Jesus, this God made man, suffers the rejection of his people, endures the passion, and embraces his cross. It may seem a dim ending to the hope and promise of the Annunciation and the Incarnation. But of course, as we know, the crucifixion is not the ending at all. It is the Resurrection of Christ and the coming of the Holy Spirit at Pentecost that lends joy to all these other events — and, in fact, the whole season of Lent.

Yet, how do we celebrate the Annunciation and the Incarnation at a time when our focus is turned squarely on the penitential rigors of Lent? Are we not almost stuck with this variety of images, potentially confusing and distracting us? On the contrary! Mary's "Be it done unto me according to your word" is reflected in the Lenten journey. Although we have many lovely images of Christmas, including genteel animals, worshipping shepherds, singing choirs of angels, and gifts from the three kings, we know that Mary's yes to God also brought upon her much difficulty and suffering.

Mary's response to Gabriel was rooted in a desire to do the will of God. Many of us, like Mary, became parents because we were open to it as the will of God. At times we may hear criticism from others or find a lack of sympathy because it was "our choice" to have children ... or to have "so many" children. Yes, on the one hand, it was; in the same way Mary's "be it done unto me" was also a choice. But for those who want to do the will of God, "choice" doesn't adequately convey what it means to be parents. Children are a gift, as was Jesus to Mary. But children also bring with them adversity, and we know Mary's suffering endured because of her compassion with her son in the midst of his own suffering.

The willingness to accept children, knowing that it will make life harder for us, is indeed a sacrifice, even when it is what we desire as we try to align our will to God's. In other words, the Incarnation and Annunciation are very much related to the season of Lent. In becoming human, Jesus took upon himself all the burdens of humanity. And if Jesus knew what it was to have a loving mother, he also knew what it was to be spat upon, scourged, and crucified. Mary was able to experience the joy of holding her child in her arms and caring for him, but she also held his dead body in her arms after his crucifixion.

That is life. We are given our own gift of life and entrusted with the lives of our children. We should expect parenting to bring us trials, as do many "choices" that we make in trying to do the will of God. But, as we remember throughout the season of Lent, Jesus' passion and death are not the end; they are followed by the Resurrection. Mary's love for Jesus, like our own love for our children, extends from womb to tomb to our hope in eternal life for each of them.

## Ponder

- Have I ever complained about parenting, only to be met by the response that it was my "choice"? How did that make me feel? How is that statement true? How is it incomplete?
- How have I suffered in sharing the struggles or pain of my children? Has it brought me closer to God?
- How do I experience children as both a gift and a challenge? Are there times when I recognize the blessing of children more eagerly and times when the responsibilities seem overwhelming?

## Pray

May it be done to me according to your word. (Luke 1:38)

## Do

*Today: The Angelus*

Today is a great day to say the Angelus, if you don't already, or to focus on it more particularly today. This ancient prayer is traditionally said aloud at 6:00 a.m., noontime, and 6:00 p.m. (though you don't have to do all three!), and is a quick and beautiful prayer to incorporate into family life on a daily basis.

The Angel of the Lord declared unto Mary
R. And she conceived of the Holy Spirit.
Hail Mary …
Behold, I am the handmaid of the Lord
R. Be it done unto me according to your word.
Hail Mary …
And the Word was made flesh
R. And dwelt among us.
Hail Mary …
Pray for us, oh holy Mother of God
R. That we may be made worth of the promises of Christ.
Let us pray:
Pour forth we beseech thee, O Lord, thy grace into our hearts, that we to whom the Incarnation of Christ thy son was made known by the message of an angel, may by his passion and cross be brought to the glory of your resurrection, by this same Christ, our Lord. Amen.

# ACKNOWLEDGMENTS

While this book was written for busy parents, it was also written by a busy parent. I would not have been able to complete the project without the support and encouragement of many people. First and foremost, thank you to my husband, Jeffrey Morrow, for supporting me throughout the writing process, including discussing certain Scripture passages with me and sacrificing his own work time for me to be able to write and edit.

Secondly, thank you to my children, without whom I would not have been able to write this book! I consider each one to be a blessing; they've brought me great joy, as well as many challenges, and both of these have helped me to grow closer to God. My daily life with them inspired these reflections in many ways, and so, although they didn't assist or make my writing any quicker, I am truly grateful for them: Maia, Eva, Patrick, Robert, John, Nicholas, and Anna Therese. Additionally, I am thankful to my amazing babysitter, neighbor, friend, and unofficially adopted family member, Anna Nuñez, whose hours of childcare — including many fun trips to the zoo — allowed me the time to write this book. Thanks also to my friend Suzanne Covine, who supported me well by entertaining my kids for hours at a time so I could get some work done.

I'm continually inspired by the many good Catholic parents around me, who courageously and joyfully embrace the demands of family life. In particular I want to thank Katie Martinson, Virginia Hughes, and Holly Taylor Coolman for always providing valuable advice and encouraging support during the most difficult of times. I'm also grateful for Melissa and Jason Shanks, without whom I would not have met my husband, and who are dedicated Catholic parents who encouraged me to do this book. Dr. Ines Murzaku, the director of the Catholic Studies Program at Seton Hall University, always encourages and supports the work of her faculty, and I am thankful for that and for her model of combining parenting and the academic life.

My Rosary prayer group has been praying for this book project for several years now! And I've felt the support of their prayers keenly, as well as their kind words throughout. Thank you to all of them: Mary Brereton, Mary Fagan, Amy Giglio, Nathalie Haughey, Dawn Hickey, Sara Lancelotti, Mollie Laracy, Katie Marchesi, Diane Merkel, Cristina Spann, Fabiana Touhey, and Bernadette Young. I've also benefited from conversation with and the support of my pastor, Father Jim Spera, as well as confessors Father Carmine Rizzi and Father Daniel O'Mullane. Thank you also to everyone at Our Sunday Visitor, especially Mary Beth Giltner and Rebecca Willen, who did an excellent job in guiding me through the proposal, writing, and editing process for this book.

Finally, I continue to grow in appreciation for my childhood with my amazing siblings Jeremy Feilmeyer, Ann Ledbetter, and John Mark Feilmeyer. Our parents, Kathryn and Robert Feilmeyer, beautifully modeled fidelity and love throughout our years at home and beyond. Only recently do I appreciate the many sacrifices they made for us, and I am so grateful for these, as well as their continued support in reaching my goals throughout my adulthood. And of course, there is no better model for family life than the Holy Family, who encountered many difficulties but always sought to do God's will in the confidence of his loving kindness. The Blessed Virgin Mary, under so many titles — especially Seat of Wisdom and Perpetual Help — has been an inspiration and a patroness for me as a mother throughout the writing of this book. Thank you, Jesus, Mary, and Joseph!

# ABOUT THE AUTHOR

MARIA C. MORROW earned her Ph.D. in theology at the University of Dayton and is an independent scholar living in New Jersey with her husband, Jeffrey Morrow. She is the mother of seven children, an adjunct professor at Seton Hall University, and the author of the academic book *Sin in the Sixties: Catholics and Confession, 1955–1975.*

# You Might Also Like

## The Handy Little Guide to Lent

Here's your easy-to-read, down-to-earth introduction to what this liturgical season is all about. You'll discover, or rediscover, how to make each Lent a time of deep personal spiritual growth.

## The Handy Little Guide to Confession

In this easy-to-read booklet, you'll gain the confidence you need to return to the Sacrament of Confession, where you will experience God's mercy and unconditional forgiveness.

## The Handy Little Guide to Spiritual Communion

The suspension of Masses worldwide as an effort to control the spread of COVID-19 has many Catholics longing for Holy Communion, but even in normal times there are other reasons Catholics may be unable to attend Mass or receive the Eucharist. That's why it's more important than ever for Catholics to understand and practice spiritual communion.

**Available at OSVCatholicBookstore.com or wherever books are sold.**

## More on Lent

### The Way of the Cross with Saint John Paul II

The Way of the Cross with Saint John Paul II provides a simple but profound opportunity to practice this devotion publicly or privately, during — and beyond — the Lenten season.

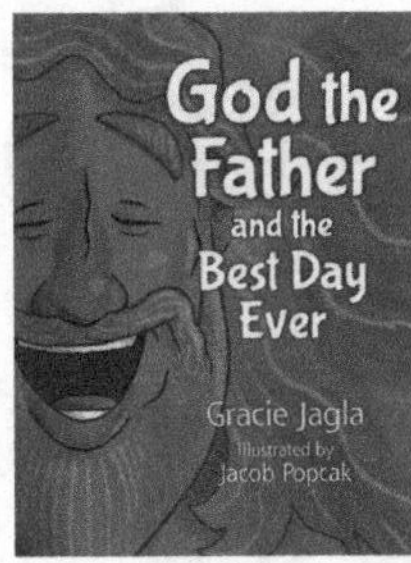


### God the Father and the Best Day Ever

With beautiful illustrations and memorable rhyme, this book tells the sweeping story of God's love for us since the beginning of time. Your child will learn how Jesus' life, death, and resurrection opened heaven, so we can spend eternity with God.

**Available at OSVCatholicBookstore.com or wherever books are sold.**